Traveling With Greyhound

On The Road for 100 Years

ROBERT GABRICK

Enthusiast Books

Enthusiast Books
1830A Hanley Road
Hudson, Wisconsin 54016 USA

Enthusiast Books are offered at a discount when sold in quantity
for promotional use. Businesses or organizations seeking details
should write to the Marketing Department, Enthusiast Books, at
the above address.

Library of Congress Control Number: 2014942911

ISBN-13: 978-1-58388-310-5
ISBN-10: 1-58388-310-X

14 15 16 17 18 19 6 5 4 3 2 1

Printed in USA

TABLE OF CONTENTS

Acknowledgements

My special thanks and deeply felt gratitude to the following individuals and institutions that helped make this book a reality.

Located in Hibbing, Minnesota, the birthplace of what would become Greyhound is the Greyhound Bus Museum. During my research and subsequent visits I have enjoyed the support, assistance, and continued friendship of Gene Nicolelli, *the* museum's driving force.

The Motor Bus Society maintains a library near Trenton, New Jersey. Joe Mahawash devoted considerable time and effort to insure access to the Society's photographs and research materials.

The Antique Automobile Club of America Library and Research Center, Hershey, Pennsylvania, provided many of the photographs prominently featured in the book.

At the time of my research visits to The Hagley Museum and Library, Wilmington, Delaware, Jon Williams, Curator of Prints and Photographs, assisted in the examination of the *Nation's Business* Collection. Marjorie McNinch, Reference Archivist, helped me research the Raymond Loewy Papers.

Kim Bravo, Librarian of the marvelous Automobile Reference Collection of the Free Library of Philadelphia, Pennsylvania, provided valuable assistance.

The Library of Congress, Washington, DC, proved to be an essential source for archival resources.

The always-supportive staff at the Detroit Public Library guided my use of the National Automotive History Collection.

John Dockendorf enthusiastically provided roadside and depot images from his expensive postcard collection.

Chris Hudson provided photographs from his collection.

Bill Luke, 90 years young, secured photographs and provided crucial information.

Barbara Markham, once again performed her long established role as valuable research partner.

While relying on the expertise and assistance of many, the responsibility for the factual accuracy and interpretations of this book are mine.

Guide for Photograph/Image Acknowledgement

AACA: Antique Automobile Club of America Library and Research Center

AC: Author's Collection

BL: Bill Luke Collection

CH: Chris Hudson Collection

FLP: Free Library of Philadelphia, Automobile Reference Collection

GBM: Greyhound Bus Museum Archives

HML: Hagley Museum and Library

JD: John Dockendorf Collection

MBS: Motor Bus Society Library

NAHC: National Automotive History Collection

Dedication

To

David Waxon and Stan Holter

Friends who preserve a valuable legacy: Owning and operating actual "antique" Greyhound Buses

Introduction

Traveling with Greyhound celebrates Greyhound's Centennial. Filled with both good fortune and misfortune, Greyhound's 100-year survival in America's dynamic and ever-changing marketplace is remarkable. Along the way, Greyhound acquired iconic status. People continue to take the "Greyhound" whenever they travel by bus. There are few illusions about the changing nature of bus travel, but Greyhound continues to be larger than life. At times bruised and battered by reality, an iconic Greyhound exists in our collective imagination; out on America's open road the Greyhound is the vehicle to experience the romance, excitement, and glamour of travel just over the ever-expanding horizon.

We go "on the road" recounting highlights of Greyhound's history aided by a series of tableaux featuring imaginary travelers grounded in real-life possibilities as they read advertisements, decide where to travel, how to manage their expenses, and ride in a variety of buses. The story of Greyhound is inextricably bound to America's story; so ride along and learn about America as seen through the windows of a Greyhound bus.

GBM

5

Chapter One
1914-1929: Starting the Engine

The Greyhound saga begins in Hibbing, a small town on northern Minnesota's Iron Range. While the area's vast forests first attracted lumbermen, the discovery of iron ore deposits led Frank Hibbing to plat a town in 1893. European immigrants and migrants from eastern states responded to the commercial development of the area's timber and mineral resources. More than 2,000 called Hibbing home by the start of the 20th century.

Looking back twenty years, *Fortune* magazine's August 1934 issue, told the "Story of the great American bus line whose name is Greyhound…The First Bus Company of the Land." Swedish immigrant Carl Eric Wickman from Hibbing, "an unvarnished young town in the Iron Range" according to *Fortune*, worked as a diamond drill operator in the open pit mines. Downtime in the mines led him to become a dealer for Goodyear tires and Hupmobile automobiles. Introduced in 1910 by Robert Craig Hupp, Hupmobile declared itself "the leader of medium priced cars." No record exists of the number of Hupmobiles Wickman sold, but he used a 1914 Hupmobile Six-Passenger Touring Car to operate "a small livery business." Such a service was of potential benefit for the vast majority of Iron Range residents who could hardly afford the typical automobile, as expensive as the average middle class house.

Wickman subsequently sold this Hupmobile for $1,200—the base price for the model—to two friends, Andy Anderson and Charles Wenberg. At a decided disadvantage, *Fortune* noted Wenberg could not drive nor speak "very intelligible English" and he soon sold his interest in the taxi service back to Wickman.

The 2014 Centennial celebration reflects what *Fortune* considered the key to the future creation of Greyhound, the 1914 decision by Wickman and Anderson to make "the innovation that changed them from taxi drivers to busmen. They decided to make the run from Hibbing to Alice, the most popular trip, on regular schedules and [charge] fifteen cents

one-way and twenty-five cents for a round trip. Business boomed."

The popularity of travel between Hibbing and Alice was rooted in necessity. When originally platted, Hibbing was thought to be south of the area's rich iron ore deposits. Discovering additional ore deposits under Hibbing, the Oliver Iron Mining Company, a subsidiary of the United States Steel Corporation decided to move Hibbing. In 1910, the company chose Alice, a mile south. A gradual process of relocation began requiring travel between the two towns. By 1919, the final move occurred with some of the old buildings towed intact. Workers cut others into sections, transported them piecemeal, and put them back together again. "Old" Hibbing, engulfed by the expanding open pit mine, gave way to the "new" Hibbing occupying the site of Alice, ending forever the run between Hibbing and Alice.

Greyhound's humble origins occurred against the backdrop of the eruption of the First World War in Europe, starting in 1914. While the United States would not officially enter the war until 1917, the government increasingly undertook an unparalleled program of government regulation and control that affected Minnesota's Iron Range. America's initial response was to supply needed war materiel—guns, trucks, and other supplies—to England and France in particular. The population of the Iron Range grew as the wartime demand for ore to supply industry increased employment opportunities.

Responding to the increased demand for bus service, Wickman, Anderson, and three additional partners created the Mesaba Transportation Company in 1916. *Fortune* called it "the first incarnation of Greyhound." By 1918, an expanding Mesaba Transportation maintained an eighteen-bus fleet that featured "homemade" bodies constructed by Wickman and Anderson mounted on White truck chassis. Wickman sold his share of Mesaba in 1922, establishing the Duluth-based Northland Transportation Company in

1925. Wickman's goal was to expand service to Minneapolis and beyond by acquiring small local service bus lines. One result of the acquisitions was a working partnership with Orville S. Caesar. In 1926, the Great Northern Railroad bought an 80-percent interest in Northland Transportation, with Wickman retaining the remaining 20 percent. Wickman and Caesar continued to manage the company, and began what *Fortune* described as "a furious campaign of expansion and more expansion," acquiring over 100 bus lines between 1926 and 1929. The two, along with other investors, then established the Motor Transit Management Company, to hold the stock of acquired bus lines and to establish Greyhound Lines.

Billing itself as the "World's Largest Motor Coach System," Greyhound established a dazzling array of subsidiaries including a number with ties to railroads. Southland Greyhound with the Southern Pacific and the Cotton Belt; Richmond Greyhound with the Richmond, Fredericksburg and Potomac Railroad; Pennsylvania Greyhound with the Pennsylvania Railroad; and replacing Northland Transportation with Northland Greyhound tied to the Great Northern Railroad. Advertisements identified additional non-railroad-connected Greyhound subsidiaries: Central, Pacific, Pickwick, Eastern, Capital, Southeastern, Western, Atlantic, Dixie, Teche, and Canadian-based Provincial Transport—later Canadian Greyhound.

While *Fortune* correctly acknowledged the leadership of Greyhound was "endowed with unusual vision," the creation of a nation-wide highway network played a crucial role in Greyhound's quest to be the "World's Largest" bus line. In 1914, when Greyhound's forerunner began service, only 750 miles of concrete highway and 3,000 miles of hard surfaced roads—gravel was considered "hard surfaced"—existed in the entire United States. Highway-based travel was arduous and the provenance of an elite—even among the wealthy—who possessed both the time to travel and the means to acquire expensive automobiles. Reflecting the arduous nature of travel, in 1915, to promote the mostly imaginary Lincoln Highway, Packard Motor Company President, Henry B. Joy took 21 days to travel from Chicago to San Francisco.

Continuing to increase the role for the government that began as a response to World War I, in 1921, Congress passed the Federal Highway Act that provided funds for the Department of Agriculture to develop a system of interstate highways. Greyhound grew as this highway network encompassed the nation, essential for Greyhound's goal to become a nation-wide bus company.

Success for Greyhound would also require more than "homemade" bodies mounted on truck chassis. The nature of the bus changed significantly contributing to improved levels of appearance, safety, comfort, and performance. Incorporated in November 1916, the Oakland, California-based Fageol Motors Company introduced the template for parlor coach buses offered by most manufacturers, the William Fageol-designed Safety Coach. The influential trade publication, *The Commercial Car Journal*, May 15, 1922, declared "New Fageol Bus Radical Departure From Conventional Design." The magazine reported Fageol "announced an inter-city motor stage, designed and built exclusively from the bumper to the tire rack." The parlor coach design featured metal body parts of aluminum, an "unusual low hung construction," a 4-cylinder Hall-Scott engine and a 68-inch wide tread "insuring absence of side sway and freedom from danger of capsizing."

Among a number of manufacturers, the White Company, Cleveland, Ohio, offered a variety of parlor coach models. Reflecting the comparisons often made to railroad equipment and modes of service, White heralded its 38- to 41-passenger capacity Model 54A as the "Pullman of the Highway." American Car and Foundry Motors Company (A.C.F.) also produced a line of buses that included parlor coach bodies. A.C.F. promotional material declared, "The Parlor Coach has been developed as the result of careful analysis of factors of luxury and comfort." The result was "dignity and fineness of appearance, beauty of line and finish." All manufacturers utilized hardwood framework for their bodies with on-the-roof baggage storage.

In addition to purchasing buses from existing manufacturers, Wickman and Caesar established a bus-building subsidiary in 1927, Minneapolis-based C.H. Will Motors Corporation. Yellow Truck and Coach, a General Motors Corporation subsidiary purchased a 30-percent interest in Will Motors in late 1929, transferring bus production for the Greyhound Corporation to its Pontiac, Michigan, facilities in 1930.

Other manufacturers developed unique bus designs in the 1920s. In 1927, prior to its acquisition by Greyhound, Pickwick stages introduced the Pickwick Observation Buffet Car combining unique design and amenities. Features included a kitchen, dining service, a radio in the observation compartment, and lavatory. Most unusual was the "glass enclosed pilot house" for the driver. Pickwick put its NiteCoach, an all-metal 26-passenger sleeping coach into service in 1928. Designed by Dwight E. Austin, the bus featured 13 compartments with upper and lower berths, a washbasin, and thermos jug. Staff included stewards and a chef. (While Pickwick usually used one word for the NiteCoach, most contemporary media sources used two words.)

Pickwick also modified a NiteCoach extending the upper bodywork to the rear bumper. In addition, Pickwick developed the bi-level 53-passenger Duplex, designed for "day travel only." Despite these variations, the basic parlor coach design continued as the industry standard for intercity bus service until the introduction of Greyhound's Super-Coach, the revolutionary Yellow Coach Model 719, in 1935.

As bus design and the very definition of the motor bus industry evolved in the 1920s, the industry looked to two models for guidance: railroads and passenger ship lines. Both models offered class-based service. Buses, however, lacked the space to offer different levels of service. As a result, bus lines eventually abandoned class-based service, opting to provide affordable transportation for the masses. The very use of the terms "coach" and "parlor coach" for buses represented efforts to apply the railroad model to buses. Reflecting the design of railroad cars, these buses often featured rear observation vestibules. While incorporating the metal grille work, signs, awnings, and lights found on railroad cars, they lacked access to the bus interior, often carrying only spare tires. A ladder provided access to the roof for baggage storage, since there was limited stowage space inside the bus.

In 1928, a Yelloway System bus crossed the United States from Los Angeles to New York, reflecting both the development of the nation's highways and the improvements in bus design. Operating primarily on the west coast, Yelloway, owned by Wesley E. Travis, competed with Charles F. Wren's Pickwick Stages. To help achieve its goal to establish a "national network of lines, cooperating through a mother com

pany," Wickman, Caesar, and Glenn W. Traer, Jr., of investment firm Lane, Piper, and Jaffray purchased Yelloway in 1929, with control moving to a New York-based financial group that created the Greyhound Corporation in 1930. Greyhound, allied with the Southern Pacific Railroad, subsequently created Pacific Greyhound to operate Yelloway, Pickwick, and the Southern Pacific's own bus subsidiary.

In its efforts to become a "national network of lines, cooperating through a mother company," Greyhound benefited from the national culture that developed in the 1920s. Key characteristics of that culture included a shorter workweek, more leisure time, higher incomes, a significant increase in the production and availability of consumer goods, access to credit that enabled immediate rather than deferred gratification, an expansion of the middle class, increased urbanization, and new roles for women. Because of these cultural changes, travel, no longer just a necessity, offered access to new places and new experiences for more people, developments Greyhound favorably exploited.

As the 1920s ended, *The Greyhound Traveler*, March 1929, published for the Greyhound customer, offered the corporate perspective, acknowledging the changing nature of travel, bus design, and the role of those "endowed with unusual vision"—unnamed but assuredly Wickman and Caesar.

"It was not a great many years ago that the motor bus was regarded as a necessary evil—to be used as a means of travel only when one wanted to go to some out-of-the-way, off-the-beaten-path town or rural community which was not graced with any of the more comfortable passenger carriers. At the time, few people saw any future for this little 'upstart industry' and as a matter of fact few people cared to see any future in it. Yet there were people—not many, but some—who, endowed with unusual vision, prophesied that this infant industry moving jerkily and uncertainly over the roads was bound somewhere. They said that one day it would grow up and glide smoothly over every highway in the nation."

The Greyhound Traveler continued, "Today the motor bus is…a masterpiece in mechanical engineering which rolls smoothly and dependably over the highways—serving thousands of rural communities as it travels between all of the nation's principal cities."

TRAVELER TABLEAU: MICHAEL

Michael is a writer. He took an extensive motor coach trip that resulted in a currently popular book. For a good portion of his travels he chose a Pickwick NiteCoach. Offering a new level of luxury for motor coach travel, the 26-passenger sleeping coach featuring 13 compartments with upper and lower berths that included a washbasin and thermos jug, and stewards and a chef entered regular service in 1928.

Michael sought creative ways to describe his travels for the armchair traveler—unlikely to take such an extensive trip. The terminals and depots became fascinating wharf-like

ports of call, the NiteCoach—an ocean liner, and the driver became the liner's captain. Beckoning the traveler to join him, Michael wove a tapestry of romance and adventure with visits to intriguing ports of call and marvelous man-made and natural wonders. He took them on a nationwide excursion of which they could only dream. Here was Los Angeles and San Francisco, the spectacular coast of California, giant Redwoods, Yellowstone Park and Old Faithful, the Grand Canyon, and the Alamo. He wove a delightful account about the glorious plantations of Dixie,

North Carolina's Outer banks, the monuments and memorials and the Capital in Washington, D.C., the hustle and bustle of fabled New York City, the rugged shorelines and forests of New England, the bucolic countryside of the Midwest, the badlands of South Dakota, and the grand vastness of Montana.

Often left out of Michael's account were the less attractive aspects of motor coach travel in the late 1920s. America's highway system was a work in progress. Most roads were unimproved. While improved highways could be concrete, macadam, or asphalt, many were only gravel or dirt—grading and leveling meant they were "improved." The frequent stops required for food, refueling, and rest room visits exposed the less than ideal roadside accommodations endured by 1920s travelers.

However, Michael's depiction of travel by motor coach helped begin the transformation that Greyhound's future advertisements would promote. Greyhound proclaimed travel was for more than necessity. Greyhound advertising encouraged people to dream and make travel an exciting and fun-filled journey; and most importantly, to make people believe they could fulfill those dreams by going Greyhound.

A 1920s Photo Album

THE TRANSITION TOURING CAR TO ENCLOSED BUS
THE FIRST INTERCITY BUS
— 1916 WHITE —

- 1916 Model — WHITE
- White Truck Co., Cleveland, Ohio
- 12 Passenger Capacity
- 30 Horsepower
- 18 feet long — 6½ feet wide
- 3,800 pounds
- Built on ¾ ton Truck Chassis
- Leather Seats

In spite of the handicaps of right-of-way, motor breakdowns, tire blowouts and leaky radiators, the bus business continued to expand. During the transition from touring cars to enclosed buses the White truck chasis with custom-built body was introduced. In 1916 the Mesaba Transportation co. was organized.

And so Greyhound began . . .

Carl Wickman and Andy Anderson purchased a 1916 White for their first commercially manufactured bus. Prior to that, the two mounted homemade bodies on truck chassis. In 1916, they also created the Mesaba Transportation Company, a major step in the creation of Greyhound. *GBM*

To commemorate thirty years of service since its purchase by Carl Wickman and Andy Anderson, in 1946 Greyhound paired the 1916 White with a famed Silversides, manufactured by General Motors Corporation in 1941. *GBM*

In 1922, Fageol introduced the revolutionary William Fageol-designed Safety Coach, the template for parlor coach buses offered by most manufacturers and used by virtually all bus lines. The low-slung chassis and wide tread gave the bus a low center of gravity, hence more stability. All Fageol buses and trucks sported unique razorback hood louvres. *NAHC*

Three Fageol Safety Coaches load up for a chartered trip outside South High School, Minneapolis, Minnesota, during the 1920s. Atop the second and third buses, men are loading large closed baggage compartments. In general, parlor coach buses usually provided on-roof baggage storage and tarps for protection from inclement weather. *GBM*

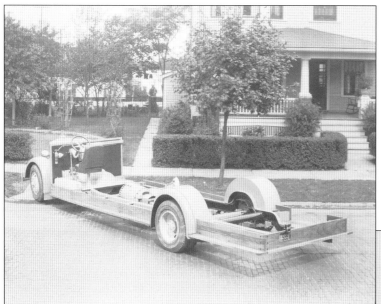

While featuring an unusual setting, this photograph provides a clear view of a 1925 parlor coach chassis. The wood framing is indicative of the extensive use manufacturers made of wood for the structural framework for metal-clad bus bodies. *HML*

Two Fageol Safety Coaches pause on Faribault, Minnesota's, Main Street in circa 1926. Each bus utilizes a different body, but evident are the revolutionary design features of the Fageol Safety Coach. *GBM*

Greyhound created its own bus-manufacturing subsidiary, C.H.Will Motors Corporation in 1927. Yellow Truck and Coach Manufacturing Company, a General Motors Corporation subsidiary, acquired a 30-percent interest in Will, transferring bus manufacturing for Greyhound to its Pontiac, Michigan, facilities. Shown is an example of a 1928 Will Parlor Coach. *AACA*

Bus body manufacturers utilized the Fageol Safety Coach chassis to develop intra-city buses. The taller body provides headroom for passengers to walk to their seats, while the solid rubber tires and the lack of luggage storage confirm its intended use. *GBM*

The Garford Motor Truck Company produced its first truck in 1908 and its first bus chassis, the KB Motor Bus chassis, in 1925. An earlier Garford truck chassis, shown in 1925, features a body based on the Fageol Safety Coach design. The Range Rapid Transit Company operated on Minnesota's Iron Range. Garford had no connection with Greyhound, but used the term to identify its motor coach chassis. *GBM*

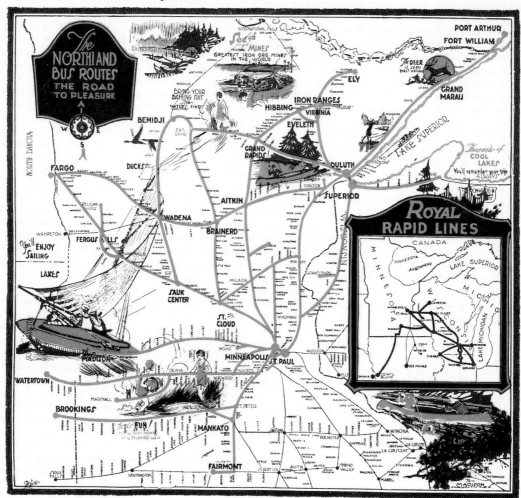

To the VACATION LANDS
of the NORTH

FROM CHICAGO northward into Wisconsin's Land of Lakes and Minnesota's Arrowhead Country, reaches the vast motor transit system of Royal Rapid Lines and the Northland Transportation Company. New, modern, all-steel buses operate on frequent schedules both day and night to every section of this glorious country. Fares are low. Service is unexcelled. Skilled, safe drivers pilot all the buses. Tickets and information at all Greyhound bus depots. For literature write Northland Transportation Company, Minneapolis, Minnesota.

NORTHLAND TRANSPORTATION COMPANY

ROYAL RAPID LINES

Carl Wickman established the Duluth-based Northland Transportation Company in 1925 and expanded service to Minneapolis and beyond by acquiring small local service bus lines. This Northland advertisement illustrates the network of lines the company established, extending into North and South Dakota. In 1926, the Great Northern Railroad bought an 80-percent interest in Northland Transportation, while Wickman retained the remaining 20 percent. *MBS*

Yelloway System operated this White Motor Company version of the Fageol Safety Coach. The bus features the configuration established by the Fageol Safety Coach. Company advertising claimed, "White builds the most dependable bus that engineering experience is capable of." *HML*

Clearly based on the Fageol Safety Coach design, this Will Motors bus features the unique elongated radiator surround common to Will buses. The opening for the hand crank for manually starting the engine is visible just below the "WMC" bumper medallion. *AACA*

This Yelloway System 1927 A.C.F. Parlor Car boasted "Coast to Coast Service." Reflecting the ever-expanding national highway network, a Yelloway A.C.F. bus crossed the continent from Los Angeles to New York. According to A.C.F., "The success of the Parlor Car type of coach has been largely due to the extremely attractive appearance, inviting patronage by appealing to a larger group of prospective passengers." *AACA*

The 1927 Pickwick Stages Observation Buffet Car offered travelers a unique design and amenities including a kitchen, dining service, a radio in the observation compartment, and lavatory. Most unusual was the "glass enclosed pilot house" for the driver. *MBS*

Bus lines sought to provide class-based service with uniquely designed buses. Pickwick's all-metal NiteCoach entered service in 1928. Designed by Dwight E. Austin, the bus featured 13 compartments with upper and lower berths, a washbasin, and thermos jug. Stewards and a chef provided services for the 26 passengers. *HML*

Pausing for a "photo-op" is a 1928 Will Parlor Coach. Based on the template established by the Fageol Safety Coach introduced in 1922, this version, operated by Greyhound Lines, features on-the-roof baggage storage as well as the railroad observation car-inspired vestibule at the rear of the bus body. Unlike the railroad car, the bus vestibule was purely decorative. *GBM*

The Greyhound Traveler, first introduced in 1929, promoted travel by Greyhound. The magazine constituted a multi-page advertisement offering highlighting the trips and destinations available by going Greyhound. *MBS*

Carl Wickman and Orville Caesar established the Motor Transit Management Company, to hold the stock of acquired bus lines and to establish "Greyhound Lines including the Yelloway System." This August 1929 advertisement by Motor Transit Management offers a tableau of "Master Seven-Years-Old," traveling alone from a "west coast city to Chicago." However, no one need worry since this "tiny incident…mirrors public faith that Greyhound men guard zealously over every mile." *GBM*

Chapter Two
1930s: Transformation by Design

For the most part, optimism for the future and the promise of unbounded opportunities combined with ever-expanding economic growth and prosperity define our view of the 1920s. In contrast, the 1930s brought with it an economic disaster that seemed to threaten the very fabric of American life. The Great Depression that followed the stock market crash of October 1929 was the most severe economic crisis in United States history. From 1929 to 1933, net income from manufacturing in the United States fell by more than two-thirds. Over 86,000 businesses failed between 1930 and 1932. Average family income that had been about $2,900 in 1929 was below $1,600 in 1932. Greyhound felt the impact of the Great Depression, with operating revenues 27-percent lower in 1932 compared to 1930.

Because it acquired the C.H. Wills Motor Corporation, the General Motors Truck Company became a major bus supplier to Greyhound starting in the 1930s. Greyhound's survival was essential to continued bus manufacturing by General Motors. As a result, the corporation took over $1,000,000 of Greyhound debt. No matter how beneficial, Greyhound's survival depended on more than this financial assistance.

The "more" was the belief by Greyhound's leadership that the challenges of the Great Depression presented opportunities. The ability to marshal the needed material and human resources to develop creative and innovative responses enabled the company to overcome the rough economic "roads." This is especially evident in five key areas: Greyhound advertising, its efforts to transform the roadside, bus design and development, terminal and depot architecture, and the links it established with the marvelous fairs and expositions designed to display optimism for the future.

The transformation *The Greyhound Traveler* described in 1929 involved the ability to transform why people traveled. If bus lines and service were to expand, let alone survive, despite the Great Depression, reasons other than necessity would have to prompt bus travel. Increasingly, people traveled for

pleasure—the opportunity to visit family and friends or take a vacation. As the Depression waned, income among the working class increased. The availability of wealth for discretionary spending encouraged people from this class to spend some of that income for leisure activities that involved travel.

Despite, or perhaps because of the serious economic difficulties of the Great Depression, Greyhound advertising in 1930s became an essential factor in the company's success. Advertising agencies developed a unique form of advertising for many products and services that blurred the distinction between needs and wants and taught people to become consumers with "the imagination and emotion to desire," as one proponent put it. While improved buses and a developing national highway network provided concrete reality, Greyhound's advertising utilized this new format, transforming the reasons to travel; recasting the entire experience of traveling by bus in highly idealized terms.

In *Advertising the American Dream*, Roland Marchand argues, that in responding to advertisements, "People preferred to identify with portrayals of themselves as they aspire to be." Greyhound advertising offered consumers not realistic portrayals—a very unappealing prospect during the Great Depression—but portrayals of aspiration. Bus transportation for the masses became more desirable in large part because Greyhound advertising successfully created an essentially mythical world for the traveler, romanticizing the trip, glamorizing the destination, and promising an ambiance of fun, excitement, and adventure.

For Greyhound, potential travelers could imagine they were in fact the mythical persons depicted in the advertisement. All of this produced an air of unreality given the Great Depression, but advertising is about what we like to think we are, not what we actually are. Advertisements that present reality cannot successfully compete with advertisements that offer the consumer larger-than-life fantasy.

A 1930s GREYHOUND ADVERTISING ALBUM

Transforming Why People Travel

An album of Greyhound advertisements from the 1930s illustrates essential themes. Advertisements usually combined more than one of these themes in an effort to persuade consumers to "Go Greyhound."

Daydreams

Marvelous advertisements tapped into what Greyhound believed potential customers wanted, believed, and even fantasized. Greyhound promised adventure, excitement, fun, education, new social relationships, comfort, safety, and an encounter with the romantic open road. The destinations are almost infinite—and Greyhound is the "vehicle" to make dreams come true. It would be a mistake to consign daydreams to mere unrealized fantasy. According to Jerome Singer, daydreams "represent rehearsals and 'trial actions for all practical future activity.'" Greyhound advertising contributed to dreams *and* to making them come true.

To go by bus is to "travel the open road." This May 17, 1930 *Saturday Evening Post* advertisement has begun to focus on "romance," a recurring theme and a way to frame a consumer's daydreams. "Like a moving picture, all the romance of the scenic highways, all the interesting panorama of village streets and city boulevards unfold before you when you travel by Greyhound bus or stage." While of far less concern to potential travelers, the advertisement indicates the Greyhound Management Company has replaced the Motor Transit Management Company. *GBM*

A visit to the Alamo "where Texas was born!" You will see its "brown bullet-chipped walls that weathered one of the fiercest battles in American history." This 1932 advertisement declares your dream trip can be fulfilled because "a modern transportation system makes this historic shrine and many others in Texas more easily accessible than ever before." How do you travel? "You've watched these Greyhound buses purring along the highways near your home. But have you traveled this way? It's a revelation of comfort...so try Greyhound for your very next trip." *GBM*

One of the most persistent daydreams is the trip to escape the rigors of a northern winter. According to this 1935 advertisement, "Greyhound has changed the whole picture. For who wants to be a prisoner of winter, when trips to any part of America can be warm, relaxed, pleasant—and cost very little." The ride in the Greyhound bus promised "floods of clean warm air from Tropic-Aire heaters" and the destination a chance to "soak up the vital sunshine of Florida, Gulf Coast, and California." Dreams do come true, thanks to Greyhound. *GBM*

Affordability

Greyhound advertisements appealed to anyone who would *like* to travel. During the 1920s, Americans benefited from increased leisure time and greater discretionary income. This meant the possibility more people could travel for reasons beyond necessity. While the upper classes preferred class-based rail travel, Greyhound's customers became the growing numbers of the increasingly more affluent middle and working class consumers.

The advertisements also encouraged the daydreams of those who could not afford to travel in the present but who would work to enjoy this experience in the future. Such advertisements promoted character traits identified with success: ambition, hard work, and thriftiness.

"A CASH BONUS for Everyone who Travels." The illustration provides a tangible example—giving cash to a traveler, bound, perhaps, for any of the exciting destinations promoted on the wall. A further reading of the advertisement indicates the cash is really the "saving on each Greyhound bus ticket." Specifically, "Each person who traveled by Greyhound during the past year has received a cash saving (or bonus), as real and definite as though a sheaf of Greenbacks had been placed in his hand." Additional themes in the advertisement included "scenic enjoyment, good fellowship, comfort," and "convenient service." A sidebar promotes Greyhound's "impressive record of safety." *GBM*

Greyhound advertisements seldom reflected a single theme. This 1932 advertisement combines the allure of "Sunny Winter Playgrounds" with affordability. "'Ah', you sigh, 'I'm afraid I can't make it, this year!' But think it over again. When Greyhound buses make the trip from snow to warm sunshine at a saving of so many dollars...the way is made so easy!" The traveler is offered Florida or California..."In any event, get away from the cold grip of winter for awhile...and go by Greyhound. It will save you many dollars for spending at the chosen winter resort, and will leave happy travel memories." *GBM*

Social Cohesion

The Greyhound bus provided a setting for social relationships, depicting travelers as adventurous, independent, and intellectually curious; character traits deemed desirable in many daydreams. The group of travelers on the bus could almost become a family or a group of friends on a journey together. While the reality usually offered something far less than these daydreams, who would want to admit it.

"Inside this blue-and-white coach there is warmth and good cheer....Who are these Greyhound passengers? The kind of folks you are glad to know...substantial, friendly people from every walk of life." This Greyhound advertisement depicts an idealized social tableau—a bus full of well-dressed congenial passengers, many pleasantly interacting with each other, all because of the trip on a Greyhound bus. *GBM*

The Parable of the Democracy of Goods

According to Roland Marchand, "The wonders of modern mass production and distribution enabled every person to enjoy the society's most significant pleasure, convenience, or benefit." This is democracy defined in terms of equal access to consumer products and services. Greyhound sought to provide transportation for the masses and not for the elite. Yet, by creating a largely mythical world that the average person could experience, Greyhound was making the ordinary person believe they were part of the elite.

"A few years ago, winter vacations in Florida, California, or the Gulf Coast were reserved for the wealthy...too rich for the average pocketbook! Those days are over. They vanished with the beginning of Greyhound bus service to all parts of America." This advertisement offers a fable of aspiration, a mythical world of prosperity, featuring a well-dressed couple—that, as the advertisement suggests, possess an "average pocketbook." However, it is November 1933, and people are still struggling to cope with economic difficulties despite the implementation of a variety of New Deal programs to end the Great Depression. *GBM*

Women

Greyhound advertisements usually depicted women as independent (financially and socially), unmarried, and a member of the middle class. These women would in general be free from family and homemaking responsibilities. In addition, women, in particular, benefited from labor-saving home appliances and other products that increased leisure time. Increasing income levels provided more discretionary income. Greyhound wanted the choice of leisure and the money available used to travel on Greyhound.

This advertisement pairs two "travelers," Columbus and a modern independent woman with discretionary income and time for a "coast-to-coast circle tour." Both explored new worlds. The potential traveler is encouraged to emulate Columbus with his spirit of adventure and the modern independent-minded equally adventurous woman. A collection of tableaux details her discoveries, including "wooded Pennsylvania mountains," a "giant redwood grove," the "rainbow-colored chasm of Arizona's Apache Trail," and the "lovely Minnesota lake country." *AC*

Men

Men in Greyhound advertisements reflected clearly identified roles including bus drivers, clerical personnel, the business traveler, pleasure traveler, and fathers in ads that featured the family. Greyhound seldom featured solitary men in its advertisements, possibly because men who traveled by Greyhound frequently do so for business and thus necessity—hardly the stuff of dreams.

This 1934 advertisement offers a series of social tableaux focusing on the male traveler. As the advertisement indicates, "Here are five of the most popular reasons for making Autumn trips by Greyhound: School travel, the Chicago World's Fair, the 'Big Game,' a business trip, and hunting and fishing." The advertisement features the restyled "pleasingly streamlined" Yellow Coach Model 788. Gone are the railroad car-inspired observation deck details. *GBM*

This advertisement reflects a number of themes Greyhound sought to promote, but the illustration focuses on well-dressed men. There is the driver, exuding competence and set apart from all others by his smartly styled uniform featuring high boots, a Sam Brown belt, and color coordinated shirt and tie. At the extreme right, a kindly grandfather holds onto his excited granddaughter's hand, while at the extreme left, a husband carries luggage as his wife has his arm. Near them are an elderly man and lastly a young man carrying skis talks with a service-uniformed Black man. *GBM*

The Highway Traveler, Greyhound's promotional magazine, featured this fisherman readying his gear, a decidedly male activity. A bright sun promises a glorious day and a full creel made possible by going the Greyhound way. *MBS*

BUSES

Greyhound advertisements invariably featured buses, promoting their safety, comfort, reliability, and modern design/style. The bus represented the latest—modernity embodied in metal, rubber, glass, and fabrics. As one advertisement put it, "It is Greyhound's pride to lead in modern, spic-and-span equipment."

The latest in modernity—the Parlor Coach-bodied Greyhound, earns the respect, admiration, and endorsement of a cross-section of not rich or poor, but middle-class travelers. Each identifies various themes: savings, comfort, fun, courtesy, and convenience. The advertisement highlights the characteristics of these "six average people, neither poor nor wealthy" folks, but for whom "dollars count." They are also "Sufficiently modern to accept new ideas, new conveniences" and a bus that "fits into modern life like hand into glove." *GBM*

Your wife and child—representing those you love and care about—are riding in the latest version of the Parlor Coach bus. Don't worry, they are comfortable and secure, as the ad touts: "Next to mental ease comes bodily comfort, found in cushioned chairs which can be adjusted to three positions—in a cheering flow of warmth from Tropic-Aire heaters." In addition, "fares are dollars lower." *GBM*

26

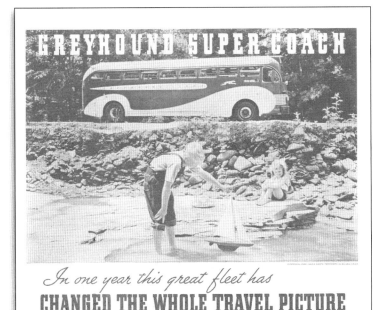

Greyhound heavily promoted its new Super-Coach, introduced in 1937. This advertisement declares, "In one year this great fleet has changed the whole travel picture." For those who wanted to know more about these new modern buses could write for a "bright colorful booklet telling about the all new Super-Coach and its innovations." *GBM*

Greyhound's "Famous modern Super-Coaches are miracles of smooth riding—healthfully heated and ventilated" are the means to the "health-giving sunshine on gay Florida beaches, along the warm Gulf Coast, through the romantic Southwest, or in colorful California." If you cannot "spare time for a southern vacation," ride the Super-Coach for Christmas and New Year for "happy reunions with family of friends." No need to daydream, "Greyhound will make these thrilling realities, at a very minimum of time and expense." *GBM*

Traveler Tableau: Helen

It's 1931. Deep into the economic storm of the Great Depression, 20-year-old Helen, a single teacher in a one-room school in rural Minnesota, needs to travel from her home near Wyoming, Minnesota, to attend summer school at the University of Minnesota-Duluth. Like many Americans, Helen has serious concerns over the economy. The local school district, in an effort to counter the Great Depression's impact and adjust expenses to match the decline in tax revenues, had reduced her salary. While necessity dictates Helen's travel, her limited budget will allow her to spend a few extra days in Duluth before her return to teaching in the fall.

A Northland Lines bus, owned by Greyhound, will take Helen up famed Highway 61 from Wyoming to Duluth, on the shores of Lake Superior.

Two examples of Greyhound's promotional magazine depict the early 1930s female traveler—glamorous role models for Helen filled with a sense of adventure, eager to be a better teacher, and excited to see the sights of Duluth and awe-inspiring Lake Superior. In the years that followed, Helen's 1931 summer would become part of her family's lore and legend.

MBS

MBS

MBS

A 1930s ROADSIDE ALBUM

Transforming the Travel Experience: Greyhound and the American Roadside

A month after its story on Greyhound, *Fortune*, September 1934, covered "The Great American Roadside." Just as today, travel then involved periodic stops to refuel the bus and allow passengers to "stretch their legs," visit the rest room, and buy food, souvenirs, and postcards. In fact, Greyhound needed to stop for refueling approximately every two hours. *Fortune* saw the roadside as "a mighty market place, 900,000 miles in length, $3,000,000 in girth." Highlighted foods sold along the "Great American Roadside" included hot dogs, beer, candy, ice cream cones, and "frozen sweets stuck to little wooded sticks" made by the Good Humor Company and the Popsicle Corporation, common fare at today's convenience stores.

The star "character" of the story of the "Great American Roadside" was the "restlessness of the American people." However, in telling the story of the "Great American Roadside," *Fortune* identified four additional characters, all linked by America's restlessness. The "American continent" became the stage upon which the drama of travel played out. Greyhound's role was to offer the continent's treasures to the traveling public. The "American people," the second character, embodied restlessness and a capacity for wonder. Greyhound promoted the traveler's "capacity for wonder" in romanticized advertisements offering glamorous travel and destinations. *Fortune's* third character was the automobile; the primary means to satisfy the people's restlessness. At the time of the writing of the article, 100-million Americans operated eight-million cars. Greyhound hoped to persuade people to "Go the Greyhound Way" and ride the bus to enjoy the scenic and historic wonders of the continent.

The "Great American Road," the fourth character—"Roads of Romance" as Greyhound characterized them—made everything in the story of the "Great American Roadside" possible. The article also noted that on the road, Americans increasingly favored "motion with the least possible interruption," suggesting the current compulsion—that the destination is the end and all else, the means—predates the passage of the Federal Highway Act of 1956, and the current Interstate system.

Greyhound sought to transform the actual travel experience, in a sense to make the reality conform more closely to the mythical world of its advertising. The quality of roadside amenities was crucial to persuading people who daydreamed about a special travel experience and then actually take the trip. In May 1937, *Bus Transportation* magazine covered Greyhound's efforts to address the most common customer concerns—food and restroom quality. In 1937, Greyhound created Greyhound Travel Stations, Inc., in an ambitious and overly optimistic effort to improve the "582 rest and lunch stops on their 30,000 mile system." Initial plans unrealistically called for establishing 3,500 diners system-wide by 1942. By 1939, the company did establish some Greyhound Post Houses, with the intent to provide loans for "lunch and comfort stops owners to provide quality foods" and "sanitary and adequately equipped rest rooms."

Lebanon, Missouri. *JD*

Clearlake Highlands, California. *JD*

Ash Fork, Arizona. *JD*

Baxter, California. *JD*

Victorville, California. *JD*

Painted Desert Park, Arizona. *JD*

Salome, Arizona. *JD*.

Irish Hills, Michigan. *JD*

Pontiac, Illinois. *JD*

Booneville, Missouri. *JD*

Rolling Prairie, Indiana. *JD*

Flat River, Missouri. *JD*

Galeton, Pennsylvania. *JD*

A 1930s TERMINAL ALBUM
Transforming the Bus Terminal: Creating Portals to New Worlds

The terminal was the first place where the mythical world created by Greyhound advertising met reality. Greyhound wanted to offer the traveler an experience that would continue the myth. To that end, it developed, and implemented as much as possible, a coherent design aesthetic for its terminals, transforming them—as its advertising declared—into distinctive "portals" to a "brand new world." However, as a nation-wide system it could not design and build every terminal. The great variety of terminals, depots, and bus stops, shown in the following album ultimately reflects Greyhound's limited opportunities to determine architectural design.

Greyhound terminals designed and constructed in the 1930s reflected what has been variously labeled Art Deco—a term not used at the time, but that has become the contemporary label of choice—Streamline, and Moderne. These labels represent an effort to categorize various 1930s architectural elements. Notice the emphasis on the horizontal aspect, including: bands of windows, often set within decorative ribbons; glass block windows; various round window frames, rounded not sharp-edged corners; distinctive signage and marquees; the running dog logo, and if you see them in color— often in glorious blue.

Note that while not all photographs date from the 1930s, each depot or terminal shown was either built or in use in the 1930s. *JD Collection*

Safford, Arizona. *JD*

Pasadena, California. *JD*

Benson, Arizona. *JD*

Banning, California. *JD*

Weed, California. *JD*

Spartanburg, South Carolina. *JD*

Columbus, Georgia. *JD*

Lake City, Florida. *JD*

La Grange, Georgia. *JD*

Brainerd, Minnesota. *JD*

Muskegon, Michigan. *JD*

Klamath Falls, Oregon. *JD*

Kalamazoo, Michigan. *JD*

Austin, Texas. *JD*

Detroit, Michigan. *JD*

Old Concord, California. *JD*

Beaumont, Texas. *JD*

Louisville, Louisiana. *JD*

A 1930s Bus Album

Transforming Buses: Modernity in Motion

Ultimately, "going the Greyhound way," meant a ride on the bus. Just as the Fageol Safety Coach revolutionized bus design in the 1920s, in the 1930s Greyhound assumed leadership for revolutionary bus designs—symbols and actual manifestations that matched the rhetoric of its advertisements. Working with General Motors, Greyhound developed buses that continue to provide the basic configuration for current buses. Streamline design represented the new transformational face of modernity.

Such efforts seem to defy common sense. Retrenchment in severe economic difficulties should be required. Instead, bold creative action became the norm. In *Twentieth Century Limited*, Jeffery Miekle notes that manufacturers relied on industrial designers in order to survive the devastation of the Great Depression, transforming the appearance of products ranging from home appliances to buses.

In particular, Greyhound played a crucial role in the development of a revolutionary new bus, the X-1, placed in test-run service in 1935. Greyhound also placed two additional experimental models, the X-2 and X-3, in service. Greyhound worked with the Yellow Coach Division of General Motors Truck Company to combine bold styling and innovative engineering to transform the motor coach. *Bus Transportation* called it the "Super Greyhound." The X-1 changed the game, forever—it remains *the* template for motor coach design.

Using the X-1 as a template, Greyhound and Yellow Coach introduced the 1936 Model 719 Super-Coach and the Model 743 Super-Coach in 1937, buses that would stylishly represent Greyhound until the introduction of their planned replacement, the iconic Silversides, starting in 1940.

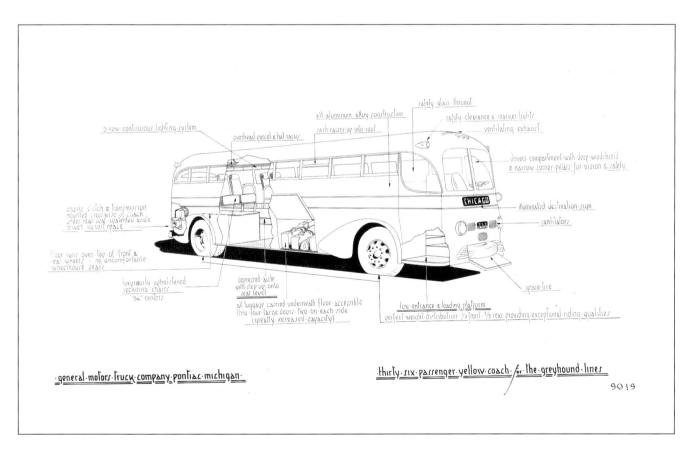

The X-1. *MBS*

Starting in 1930, Greyhound operated the bi-level 53-passenger Duplex, a redesigned Pickwick NiteCoach, for "day travel only." The Pickwick Motor coach works, Inglewood, California, extended the upper bodywork to the rear bumper on the Duplex for added passenger capacity, while continuing passenger compartments. *CH*

Yellow Truck and Coach introduced the Type 250 parlor coach in 1930. This example displays the purely decorative features of the railroad observation car vestibule. It lacks access from the bus interior, and is too narrow to provide space to stand and "observe." The marker lights and the metal awning complete the expected design elements. The ladder provides access to the roof for luggage storage. *MBS*

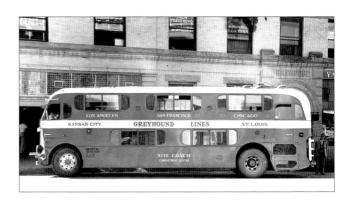

Greyhound inaugurated Night Coach service in 1933 on a new version of the original Pickwick NiteCoach introduced in 1928. This 1936 advertisement for the "Streamlined easy riding parlor coaches" declares, "Soft-cushioned chairs by day are converted into full-sized, comfortable births at night. Dressing and wash-rooms are provided. Light lunches are served aboard. A courteous porter is at your service all the way." *MBS*

Greyhound added parlor coach models to its fleet that no longer featured railroad car vestibules. For 1934, Yellow Coach promoted the "pleasingly streamlined" styling of the Model 788. The bus still used tarp covered roof cargo storage accessed by an attached step and ladder. *AACA*

While exterior styling garnered the most exposure in Greyhound advertising, travelers spent their time inside the bus. This view, intended to impress potential travelers, provides a look at the interior of a parlor coach. Those seats look very comfortable. Visible is the increased overhead interior luggage storage of the later models. *AACA*

Built in 1935 for Greyhound by the Yellow Coach Division of the General Motors Truck Company, the revolutionary X-1 represented the future of the motor coach. The bus diverged significantly from existing parlor coach models. Extensive use of aluminum resulted in a vehicle more than 2 tons lighter with increased fuel economy, a decided payoff. While it looked taller, the X-1 was actually 2 inches lower. A transversely-mounted engine located under the rear seats eliminated the hood and extra length of front-mounted engine configurations. Elevated seating provided space for two baggage compartments eliminating the less-than-desirable roof top storage. *AACA*

Greyhound called the Model 719 the "Super-Coach," its lineage with the X-1 "family" visibly evident. Acknowledging the "new conception of design" of the "blunt-nosed, modernistic vehicle in the familiar blue-and-white greyhound colors," *Automobile Topics*, August 17, 1936, declared it was "One of the most significant developments in motor bus transportation." *AACA*

Only a year later, in 1937, Greyhound introduced the Model 749 Super-Coach. Characterized by only minor styling changes from the Model 719, the bus now featured two rear windows and revised rear-end grillwork and front-end details. The ventilation grille above the next-to-last side window indicates the bus shown is a later air-conditioned equipped version. *AACA*

Greyhound recognized the advantages of capitalizing on opportunities for promotion using its buses for special events: Camp Fire Girl outings, bathing beauty contests, and special appearances of Santa Claus. In particular, the swimsuit-attired women flank Johnny Weissmuller, Olympic medalist and star of *Tarzan* movies. *AACA*

A 1930s Fairs and Expositions Album
Transformation on Display

The 1930s featured a stunning series of fairs and expositions. They reflected the other side of the 1930s, celebrating the glorious potential of the future, optimistically focusing with tremendous creativity on alternatives to the despair and hopelessness of the Great Depression. Greyhound extensively promoted travel to these events, creating special equipment and exhibits to publicize its own innovative responses to difficult economic conditions. In a way, Greyhound's efforts were proof that the world created in its advertisements was in fact more real than fantasy. *Aspiration* was part of the very core of Greyhound; success came because the company believed it would succeed.

MBS

MBS

A Century of Progress

The first fair was "A Century of Progress," opening in Chicago for a two-year run starting officially on June 1, 1933. Publicity characterized the 424-acre fair as a "dream city." Greyhound promoted travel to the Century of Progress and provided 60 Intra-Fair buses—tractor-trailer units—developed by General Motors Truck Company, Pontiac, Michigan, for travel inside the fair. Greyhound offered replicas of the "stream-line trailer type buses" for $1.00. Greyhound's June/July 1933 *Highway Traveler* magazine offered a sixteen page *Visitors Guide*. For the Fair's second year, Greyhound offered a special "World's Fair Travel Number."

TRAVELER TABLEAU: ANDREW

Relaxing after a demanding day at work, a *Saturday Evening Post* advertisement catches the eye of Andrew who works in a factory assembling farm machinery in Racine, Wisconsin. "ON TO CHICAGO. YOU'D BETTER BE THERE! The greatest World's Fair of history is sparkling in three miles of surpassing beauty, beside the blue waters of Lake Michigan." Intrigued by the advertisement's illustration depicting "The Electrical Group" that floats like a "dream city in a sea of colored lights," Andrew plans to take advantage of Greyhound's fares that are "immensely lower than other first class transportation." In addition, the "Tour Coupon books" entitle him to "first-class hotel accommodations, entrance to the Fair Grounds, and a great tour of Chicago, all at bed-rock prices."

MBS

Andrew has a week's vacation and has been saving for a trip for over two years. Once inside A Century of Progress, Andrew, along with the other 35,000,000 visitors, will ride specially designed Greyhound/General Motors Auto-Liners. During his stay, he plans to take advantage of the Tour Coupon books he read about in the advertisement entitling him to "first-class hotel accommodations, entrance to the Fair grounds, and a great tour of Chicago."

Travelers in 1936 enjoyed an embarrassment of riches—three expositions: The Texas Centennial in Dallas; the Great Lakes Exposition, celebrating Cleveland, Ohio's centennial; and the San Diego Exposition, officially known as the California Pacific International Exposition, in San Diego. Greyhound advertising called it "The Greatest Show on Earth!" Greyhound promised "more than childish fancy," offering "the most fascinating three-ring show in American history." For the Great Lakes Exposition, Greyhound chose to honor Cleveland's White Motor Company, for its in-fair tractor-trailer units.

Cleveland Great Lakes Exposition. *AACA*

The New York World's Fair

President Franklin Delano Roosevelt officiated at the opening the New York World's Fair on April 30, 1939, amidst the lingering effects of the Great Depression and the gathering storm clouds of war in Europe. Greyhound promoted travel by its buses to the Fair and operated large 120-passenger capacity buses and 40 three-car tractor-trains called "sidewalk-crawlers" to cover the ten miles of roads in the three-and-a-half-mile long and up-to-a-mile wide 1,216.5-acre site.

The Fair's 1939 motto, "Building the World of Tomorrow," reflected the possibilities of transforming the world into something better in the future.

Engineers and industrial designers created dynamic manifestations of utopian dreams on view for the 45-million visitors for the Fair's two-year run. Ordinary Americans generally saw these designs and the Fair's exhibits as tangible evidence of the reality of a better life for everyone.

The 18-story tall Trylon and 700-foot Perisphere, to this day are the recognizable symbols of the Fair. The Perisphere housed Democracity, the vision of the city of the future designed by Henry Dreyfuss. Futurama, General Motors' exhibit, designed by the noted Norman Bel Geddes, offered a fascinating vision of America in 1960.

1939 in-fair bus. *AACA*

1940 version. *AACA*

In addition to the World's Fair in New York, travelers could "Swing Around America! This Summer… by Greyhound" and "visit the Golden Gate International Exposition in San Francisco for $69.95." With boundless enthusiasm, the ad writer's p r o s e sought rhetorical heights that few could refuse—or so Greyhound hoped:

"Call it what you will—a fortunate conjunction of the planets, or the inscrutable march of events, or just plain good luck—but 1939 has brought to America the most amazing cycle of fun, excitement and thrills in its fast-moving history! Shining stars in this galaxy are the New York World's Fair and the Golden Gate Exposition. But sprinkled between, on this giant coast-to-coast orbit, are the scarcely lesser lights of vacation enchantment—cool and wondrous national parks, northern lakes and mountains, surf-swept beaches, dude ranches, every summer scene on the map."

The advertisement explained what the cost-conscious traveler got for $69.95. "This amazingly low rate includes transportation from your home, across the continent to one Fair, then back to the other, and return to your home—following your choice of scenic routes. You can take as long as ninety days—or the trip can easily be made in two weeks. It's an all time bargain, no matter how you plan it."

TRAVELER TABLEAU:
GERTRUDE AND LUCILLE

In 1939, single sisters Gertrude and Lucille—always called Gert and Lucy—in their twenties, want to travel together and visit the New York World's Fair. Both work as secretaries in downtown Detroit offices sharing a small apartment in a rooming house. On Fridays, after work, they meet at the Streamline Modern Greyhound Terminal on Washington Boulevard and take a Blue Goose Lines bus to their parent's farm—the bus actually stopping at the road that leads up to the family farm house. They flag the bus to stop at the same location on late Sunday afternoons and ride back to Detroit.

Among Greyhound's advertisements for the World's Fair, the sisters tacked up one torn from *The Saturday Evening Post* in their shared bedroom at the farm. They dreamed of joining "America's Millions [who] will go by Greyhound" to "an incredible dream city… stretching for miles in the fantastic designs of tomorrow's architecture, glowing with futuristic murals." While they did not fit the social tableau featured in the advertisement, Gert and Lucy still pictured themselves marveling at a visit to the Trylon and Perisphere and riding around the Fair in one of the 100 buses built by Yellow Truck and Coach which were styled by well-known industrial designer, Raymond Loewy.

Traveling to the Fair, the women rode Greyhound's Model 743 Super-Coach, introduced in 1937, and the focus of Greyhound's Fair exhibit.

NY Exhibit. *AACA*

A 1930s Highway Traveler Album

Part of Greyhound's efforts to promote interest in motor coach travel was its own bi-monthly magazine, *The Highway Traveler*. As previously noted, people prefer "to identify with portrayals of themselves as they aspire to be." Greyhound hoped that enticing covers and informative descriptions of scenic attractions and desirable destinations inside the magazine would encourage potential travelers to dream and then actually travel. The longevity of a Greyhound in-house magazine for travelers into the 1980s indicates its success.

Covers: All MBS

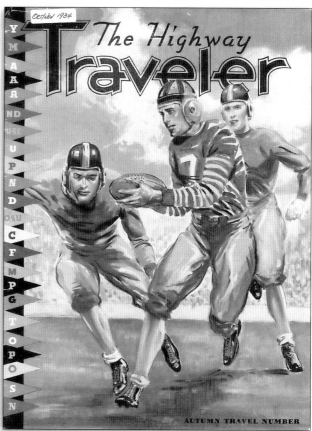

Chapter Three

1940-1952: America's "Greatest Generation": Enduring War, Enjoying Peace, Enduring War

1940-1941: Eve of War

Following the German invasion of Poland on September 1, 1939, and the declarations of war against Germany by England and France that followed, the United States government banned European travel for Americans. President Franklin Delano Roosevelt took the opportunity to proclaim 1940 to be "Travel America Year." With fanfare, Greyhound reprised its 1938 "This Amazing America" promotion declaring 1940 as "the best year in history for exploring the limitless attractions of your own country." High on the list for 19-million travelers was the

World's Fair that reopened in New York on May 11, 1940. Other destinations included San Francisco's Golden Gate International Exposition, open for its second year; "Quaint Williamsburg, Virginia... charmingly and accurately restored to its 17th Century beauty"; "the natural wonders and vacation thrills" of Canada; Key West, Florida; the Great Stone Face in New Hampshire; and the "highway through a tree in California." To take these trips in style, Greyhound offered travelers a distinctive new bus.

GBM

The Silversides

"America now has a newer, finer way to travel. It's more than a new bus—it's a new experience in highway travel." Fulfilling the promise of its exhibit at the 1939 World's Fair, in 1940 Greyhound introduced the third Super-Coach to serve in its fleet. Arguably, the most iconic, it was as distinctive from its predecessors as the first Super-Coach, introduced in 1936, was from the parlor coach model it replaced. A 1940 Greyhound promotional brochure declared, "America has a newer, finer way to travel—the recently introduced Super-Coach, new leader of Greyhound's nationwide fleet. It's more than a new bus—it's a new experience in highway travel. It's different—from its sleek streamlined alumilite-finished exterior to its restful, smartly styled, air-conditioned interior—from its retractable step at the front door to the new-type Diesel engine at the rear." Following the basic template established by the X-1, the "streamlined alumilite-finished exterior" resulted in the use of "Silversides" to distinguish it from previous Super-Coach Models. While eye-catching styling and passenger comfort would attract travelers, Greyhound also benefited from the diesel-engine fuel economy—a bottom-line concern given Greyhound's reported 1940 fuel consumption of nearly 41-million gallons.

AACA

Virtually unheard of for passenger cars, among the Silversides features that most appealed to travelers was air conditioning. Greyhound declared that the interior of the bus could be up to 35 degrees cooler than the outside temperature. Greyhound publicity also mentioned the benefits of a comfortably warm interior during the cold of winter. While Greyhound had been retrofitting previous Super-Coach models, all Silversides featured this "thermostatically-controlled" amenity when delivered fresh from Yellow Coach/General Motors.

The smartly styled alumilite clad Silversides Super-Coach, bound for the World's Fair, is paired with two equally fashionable women wearing the latest smartly styled fashions. The message is clear: the smart and fashionable (and who would aspire to be less?) go the fashionable Greyhound way. *GBM*

ACF Buses

During the early 1940s, in addition to the famed General Motors Silversides Super-Coach, Greyhound's fleet consisted of buses from other manufacturers. For example, while never used in large numbers, Greyhound purchased American Car and Foundry Motors or ACF buses, manufactured in Berwick, Pennsylvania. Their basic design reflects the template created by the famed X-1.

An ACF Model 37-P bus photographed in 1940. *AACA*

An ACF Model 37-P interior, highlighting the driver area. *AACA*

Greyhound Advertising 1940-1941: Eve of War

While war raged in Europe, Greyhound advertisements offered an inviting portrait of America still at peace, still a place to travel freely.

Prior to the introduction of the Silversides Super-Coach, Greyhound published this advertisement, featuring the 1938 Super-Coach, in an early 1940 issue of *The Saturday Evening Post*. Reflecting a kind of "It's June in January" theme, the advertisement declares the "Super-Coach will enclose a glowing cross-section of June weather, as you ride through the white magic of winter." The advertisement offers an interesting contrast between an accurate Super-Coach rendering and modernist landscape. *GBM*

It takes a team of "specialists" to help the Greyhound traveler. Greyhound took the opportunity in this 1941 advertisement to introduce the team members: the Greyhound Agent, the Greyhound Driver, the woman who sells the "*expense paid tours* [and] arranges everything," and the Greyhound mechanic. It is this superb team that supports the Silversides Super-Coach—*the* means to see "This Amazing America." *GBM*

1940-1941 Travel Brochures

Greyhound advertisements often included a mail-in coupon for more detailed travel brochures. Travelers could also stop by the numerous Greyhound Information Offices in locations including New York City, Philadelphia, Chicago, Minneapolis, Fort Worth, St. Louis, Cincinnati, New Orleans, and San Francisco. All *MBS*

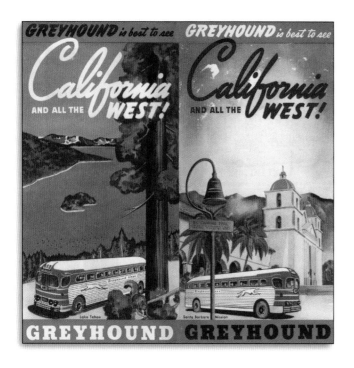

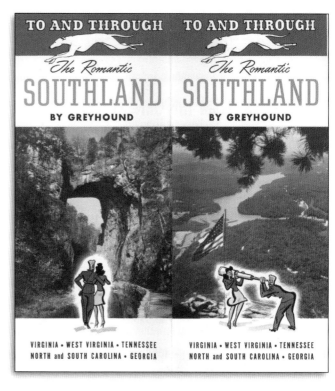

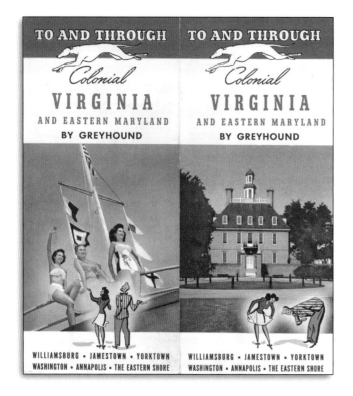

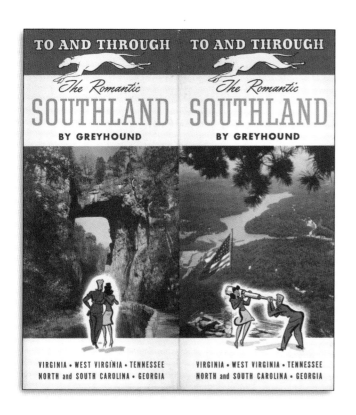

The Highway Traveler 1940-1941: Eve of War

At the start of the 1940s, and prior to American entry into World War II, *The Highway Traveler* continued to glamorize travel. However, offering an aura of mystery and allure, this cover reflects a different approach to persuading readers to go Greyhound. The smoldering look in the eyes of this *femme fatale* promises danger—and then there is that bare shoulder and cigarette. *MBS*

In sharp contrast, the bright-eyed and smiling symbol of wholesomeness is more typical of *The Highway Traveler* covers. After the big game, this is someone you can take home to Mother. *MBS*

1942-1945: Greyhound Enlists "For the Duration"

Following the Japanese attack on Pearl Harbor, December 7, 1941, America was at war. Carried out on the home front, Greyhound and the entire bus industry's support for the war proved significant. Buses moved the great majority of selectees from hometowns to induction centers. Crucial to building and maintaining morale, buses also carried military personnel home on leave and furloughs as well as relatives to camps for visits. Rationing of rubber and gasoline put a premium on travel, resulting in a significant decrease in private automobile use. As a result, in 1942, buses transported an amazing 692,000,000 passengers, compared to 396,000,000 passengers for the largest peacetime year total.

Greyhound advertising stressed both the importance of bus transportation and the company's optimism for the postwar future. Greyhound acknowledged that military priorities came first and its advertising made sure the public knew it was a shining star in the patriotic firmament of America's leading industries. One advertisement declared, "Please remember…wartime travel is not 'as usual.' The Greyhound Lines are doing everything in their power to keep essential travel on the move—and at the same time, to conserve materials and equipment vital to America-at-war."

Greyhound informed the public about its efforts, including operating at reduced wartime speeds, saving rubber, making every bus seat work full-time, eliminating charter service, except for the military, and the "bottom line"—"cooperating fully with the Office of Defense Transportation to help win the battle of transportation." The 35-mile-per-hour speed limit maximum actually resulted in greater wear on buses engineered for higher operating speeds than automobiles. Greyhound's 1942 *Annual Report* noted that overall, wartime operations costs increased by about 30 percent per mile. In addition, the reduced speeds required a complete revision of Greyhound's operating schedule—quite a task in the days before computers. Most historical accounts of the home front in World War II devote some attention to rationing—rubber, gasoline, and various food items—as they impacted the consumer. Rationing and government production regulations also presented significant challenges for Greyhound. In the late

AACA

1930s and early 1940s, yearly bus production averaged around 2,200. In 1943, all production stopped, while for 1944, the government authorized only 1,825. These curtailments put a tremendous strain on Greyhound's fleet. Parts needed for repairs were in shorter supply and older buses required extensive maintenance.

Compounding these problems was the loss of experienced Greyhound personnel: over 5,000 Greyhound employees entered military service, while others chose to take new and more lucrative jobs in plants devoted to war production. Greyhound's *Annual Reports* acknowledged one response—the increased role women played in its labor force.

Despite these wartime conditions, Greyhound continued to grow and lead the intercity motor coach industry. By 1944, *Fortune* reported Greyhound had 35 percent of the intercity bus business, a fleet of 4,000 buses, 64,700 miles of routes, and scheduled stops at some 6,000 cities, towns and villages.

While dreams were a vital theme in Greyhound wartime advertising, the company did its own dreaming, funding research and development of helicopter service. *Greyhound Looks Ahead to Integrated Air-Bus Service*, a company research study released during the war, reflected the company's optimistic belief in the future of air travel. "Long experience in transportation has given Greyhound a conviction of a growing need for the establishment of local air travel service." Greyhound planned to have helicopters designed by Raymond Loewy stop at 25- to 75-mile intervals with buses linking these locations to its larger network. While these plans never "got off the ground," they reflect Greyhound's optimistic corporate culture.

Raymond Loewy-designed helicopter model. *HML*

Raymond Loewy rendering of The Highway Traveler. *HML*

In addition to his efforts to design Greyhound helicopters, Raymond Loewy played a major role during the war designing Greyhound's postwar buses. Using its own magazine for inspiration, Greyhound christened the first new bus "The Highway Traveler." A wartime Greyhound brochure indicated the proposed bus would feature air suspension and three separate passenger compartments. News accounts' noted plans included equipping the bus with air-cooled aviation engines supplied by the Consolidated Vultee Aircraft Corporation.

The Highway Traveler 1942-1945: Wartime

The *Highway Traveler* magazine reflected Greyhound's pledge of "whole-hearted cooperation in the war effort." The June/July 1942 cover displayed the American flag and the United States Supreme Court building in the background. To promote patriotism nearly three hundred magazines took part in the "United We Stand" campaign agreeing to feature the American flag on their July 1942 covers. *MBS*

Reflecting patriotism as Greyhound's number one priority, this cover features an image of legendary William "Bull" Halsey, Jr., who at the time this issue was available—February/March 1942—was a Vice Admiral in the United States Navy serving in the Pacific. In April 1942, ships under his command would provide escort support for the famous raid on Tokyo led by James Doolittle using B-25 bombers flown off the aircraft carrier *USS Hornet*. *MBS*

This cover also patriotically acknowledges the United States Navy. *MBS*

For this issue, Greyhound offered a colorized version of the iconic Joe Rosenthal photograph of United States Marines raising the American flag on Iwo Jima. Following the war, Greyhound would generally use photographs rather than artist's illustrations for *The Highway Traveler* covers. *MBS*

The war is over and *The Highway Traveler* offers a celebratory cover featuring an iconic Silversides traveling "Victory Highways." *MBS*

A GREYHOUND ADVERTISING ALBUM
1942-1945: *Wartime*

Emblematic of Greyhound's commitment to the war effort following the Japanese attack at Pearl Harbor, this advertisement illustrates changing "just one word and you have a challenging, fighting phrase for all Americans who travel in these critical times...'SERVE America Now—so you can SEE America Later!'" The advertisement's intention is to inspire Americans to defer the dreams of pleasurable travel for a higher aspiration—"Victory." What a contrast to the 1940-1941 advertisements. *GBM*

Wartime conditions meant Greyhound really did not need to convince people to travel. Instead, Greyhound wanted to remind everyone that it was doing something significant to bring America victory in World War II—serving the needs of "America's two great armies, military and civilian" with the Greyhound Super-Coach. The mail-in coupon offered the Defense Map of America that also includes "information on military insignia, rank of officers and men." *GBM*

Dreams

While depicted as dreams, Greyhound promoted magnificent new terminals and revolutionary buses during the war—their intended actual postwar production, tangible evidence that dreams could come true in a peacetime home front.

A soldier and his girl—most likely his postwar bride, include a new Greyhound Bus terminal with helicopter service in their postwar dreams. The advertisement pays tribute to "everyone who has helped smash the Axis," including those who put up with the "discomfort and crowding" of wartime bus travel "with a smile." Everyone is a "good soldier." Also included in Greyhound's wish list are new Post Houses and "fine new motor coaches." *GBM*

In 1943, the end of the war was still a dream, "But I can dream, can't I?" says this GI. "Somewhere in the dreams of every fighting man," the advertisement declares, "are the trips he intends to make, one day, in the land he's fighting for—and, usually, one very special trip with the girl who waited!" Looking into this future, "Greyhound's post-war plans are based on making those trips everything that a man has pictured in his daydreams." *AC*

Another postwar dream—"tomorrow's 'dream bus'...coming, sure as Victory." While this dream is a soon-to-be "gleaming fluted metal, curved plastic glass" reality, this late 1944 advertisement acknowledges Greyhound has its priorities straight. Most important is the "full-time job of carrying war manpower." *GBM*

Women and Men

During World War II, Greyhound advertising featured women and men in clearly defined roles.

A long awaited "V Mail" has arrived. The three stars on the Service Flag suggest a number of possibilities. This young woman may have brothers in the service, or be a sweetheart with a loved one overseas, or a wife whose husband is in the military. *GBM*

This Greyhound advertisement features a mother with a son in the service. *GBM*

Greyhound's depiction of wives and mothers with soldier-husbands often poignantly expressed deeply held feelings. While the war would end in the coming year, Christmas, 1944, still meant Service Flags with blue stars hung in windows for millions. Addressed to the "little boy at-the-window" wearing his own uniform, the advertisement promises the "greatest homecoming ever" if everyone keeps "everlastingly at the job we're doing"—a message his mother and the wife of that "blue star" can most appreciate. *GBM*

For obvious reasons, wartime Greyhound advertisements featured men serving in the military. *GBS*

Expanded Media Messages: Radio, Movies, and Music
1942-1945: Wartime

Before, during, and after the war, Greyhound utilized radio, film, and music, as well as print media, to promote itself. On the Mutual Don Lee Network on the west coast, Greyhound sponsored "The Romance of the Highway" touting travel by Greyhound, of course. In early 1940, "This Amazing America" aired coast-to-coast on the NBC Blue Network—the title designed to coincide with Greyhound's "This Amazing America" travel promotions. The quiz show featured two teams competing to answer historical and geographic questions about America, with cash prizes for the on-air contestants and listeners, as well.

Initially appearing in films such as the widely remembered *It Happened One Night* and the less well known or regarded *Cross Country Cruise* during the 1930s, the Greyhound bus continued to "star" in films during the 1940s. Its iconic status meant a Greyhound had to be *the* bus in a film that included buses. Released in 1941, *This Amazing America*, produced by the Hal Roach Studio, featured two fictional contestants of Greyhound's actual 1940 radio program who win a trip around the country.

As this advertisement explains, during the war, service personnel "All over the World" watched *This Amazing America*. Greyhound declared the movie filled a need for the "millions in uniform" who are "dreaming about the magnificent land for which they are fighting." *GBM*

The romance of Greyhound travel was even set to music. Written in 1945, "Love on a Greyhound Bus," tells the story of two passengers who "both fell in love on a Greyhound Bus, That's us—in love on a Greyhound Bus." The song became part of *No Leave—No Love*, a 1947 MGM film starring Van Johnson and Pat Kirkwood with music provided by the bands of Xavier Cugat and Guy Lombardo. *GBM*

TRAVELER TABLEAU: CLIFF

MEMORIAL SERVICE
FRANKLIN DELANO ROOSEVELT
PACIFIC GREYHOUND SHOP
San Francisco, ONE P.M. April 14, 1945

AACA

Cliff, too old for the draft, was one of the essential civilian workers who helped America's home front industries produce the goods and services that assured victory. Cliff is among this group at a Memorial Service conducted by and for the employees of the Pacific Greyhound Shop. The nation deeply mourned the death of President Franklin Delano Roosevelt on April 12, 1945. This subsequent ceremony reflects the personal devotion and affection he engendered among the American people.

During the war, Cliff relocated from the Midwest to California, initially thinking about working in one of the factories producing aircraft or a shipyard. Over the years, he always found time to tinker with cars and trucks. The Greyhound bus ride to California got him interested in the opportunities to work as a mechanic for Greyhound. He plans to make California his home, especially since he married Marie, his sweetheart from back in the Midwest who followed him to California and works in the Pacific Greyhound Shop office. She is also somewhere in the photograph.

A GREYHOUND BUS ALBUM
1946-1952: Homecoming and Making Dreams Come True

"The Greatest Generation," as Tom Brokaw called them, had done their job—the war was over. Now service personnel from overseas were coming home, joining those on the home front anxious to fulfill the dreams that had sustained them during the difficult years of war-caused separation, disruption, relocation, and loss.

Buoyed by victory, Americans generally shared a tremendous optimism about the future—visions of a world at peace with a good job, a new car, marriage, kids, a new house, even a college education would all be possible—dreams can come true. The pent-up demand fueled an amazing postwar economic boom, as eager consumers sought to make up for the years of rationing, shortages, and the absence of consumer goods dictated by the dictates of war.

The genesis of developments that shaped the world we currently live in began in the period after World War II. Owning a car encouraged newly married GIs to own a home, purchased with the benefit of zero interest GI Bill financing, in the burgeoning suburbs. The congested morning and evening "rush hour" commute to work had begun. The Baby Boom generation was on its way.

Initially, eager just to replace the badly worn or worn out, Americans settled for products that differed little, if at all, from their wartime predecessors. Manufacturers needed time and resources to develop new products, gladly supplying consumer demand with the same or little changed products while they developed the new products they knew consumers would soon want.

Automobile manufacturers led the way starting with the startlingly different 1947 Studebaker. "First by far with a postwar car" was a prominent slogan for the South Bend, Indiana-based independent manufacturer. Ford was the first Big Three automobile manufacturer to offer a new postwar design, introducing the 1949 Ford, to the public in 1948.

Greyhound offered a slightly changed Silversides Super-Coach for postwar travelers, followed by two significant experimental prototypes in 1948 and 1949—Greyhound's initial installments in making wartime dreams come true.

Postwar Silversides

Following the war, Greyhound began to add revised Silversides to its fleet. Labor and material shortages following the war forced Greyhound to make minimal styling changes. While very dramatic when first introduced in 1940, Greyhound also sought to make much of these virtually identical "new" models. It was difficult to create excitement for one-piece front and rear bumpers that replaced those divided by center inserts or a new engine heat vent added behind the last side window. Seeking to find something to validate efforts to get people excited about the minimally altered model, Greyhound and the media made much of the restyled interiors attributed to Raymond Loewy, highlighting the use of "metal, plastic, and natural wood" as well as the new color scheme—a light blue ceiling and brown mohair seats. The use of diesel engines for these buses was of greater significance.

MBS

The Highway Traveler

Showing its intent to make the dreams it offered during the war come true, Greyhound unveiled the first of two very distinctive buses, the Highway Traveler, in the spring of 1948. The experimental prototype was equipped with a single axle rather than the dual rear axles suggested in the Raymond Loewy rendering and the variations featured in numerous advertisements. The bus was eighteen inches taller that the Silversides but the same length. The two interior seating decks held 50 passengers, up from 37, a "washroom" toilet, and water cooler.

AACA

AACA

AACA

The Scenicruiser

In mid-1949, Greyhound offered the experimental Scenicruiser, destined to become one of Greyhound's most famous buses. Built by Greyhound engineers and mechanics in the Chicago plant of General Motors, the Scenicruiser project involved the Raymond Loewy Associates and the styling section of General Motors. With its split-level design, the bus represented a sharp departure from the Highway Traveler based on the design of the experimental X-1, unveiled in 1935.

For some, the efforts to pursue the dreams in a peaceful postwar ended abruptly. Less than five years after V-J Day, August 15, 1945, military forces of Communist North Korea invaded South Korea on June 25, 1950. Working cooperatively with the United Nations, the United States entered the war that would last until July 27, 1953. In addition, while this war did not require the extensive regulations commonplace in World War II, the government limited the availability of some materials and supplies that affected automobile, truck, and bus production.

AACA

AACA

TRAVELER TABLEAU: WALLY

Wally is home after three years in the Army, serving in Italy and Germany. While enjoying victory, he is anxious to put the war behind him and work on making the things he dreamed about during the war come true. Reading an older wartime advertisement was like reading his biography. He had put "his uniform in mothballs" and slipped into some "loose easy civvies." What's more, "He and the lady he loves" found "a place to dream those old happy dreams." They plan to take a honey-moon trip on a Greyhound and start making dreams of a picket fenced-bungalow come true.

The newlyweds chose to take *the* honeymoon trip—to "spectacular Niagara Falls." This advertisement helped them "pick 'n' choose", especially after they sent in the coupon for a "full-color map and folder" that provided additional information. Going the Greyhound way meant they traveled on the iconic Silversides Super-Coach.

MBS

GBM

A GREYHOUND ADVERTISING ALBUM
Postwar: 1946-1952

Following World War II, Greyhound advertising reprised many of the themes introduced in the 1930s. Postwar ads often featured a married or soon-to-be married couple, dreaming of the bright future together after years of separation—planning their future, enjoying peace and prosperity.

Daydreams

While reflecting a number of themes, this advertisement encourages the potential traveler to dream about travel to warm winter locations and to dream you look like the swim-suited blonde-haired woman, or as a man, to dream you might meet someone as attractive as a wonderful added benefit during your travels by Greyhound. *GBM*

Wartime meant tremendous changes. The soldiers who returned were very different from those who left and they returned to a very different home front. Unfortunately, the dreams offered by Greyhound in this advertisement seek to reestablish the past and the security of tradition. Everything is in its proper mythical place: "great oaks draped with Spanish moss," and "fine old white pillared homes," a subservient black just off a box of Aunt Jemima pancake mix, and fun-loving white folks enjoying a tune strummed on the old banjo. Fortunately, this type of Greyhound advertisement was the exception rather than the rule. *GBM*

Affordability

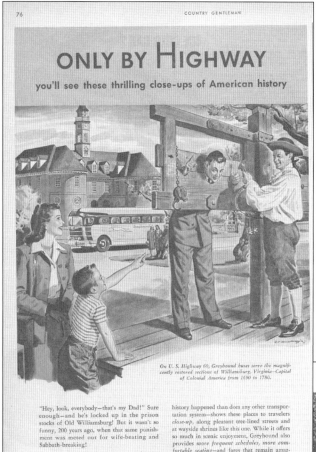

Following the war, Greyhound's customers became the growing numbers of the increasingly more affluent middle and working class consumers. An example of the "By Highway" series of advertisements, this one focuses on economical transportation for the masses, the result of "America's fine highways" and Greyhound buses that roll along them, featuring frequent schedules, comfortable seating and "amazingly low fares." *GBM*

Meet "your Greyhound agent," the man who can give the traveler "the most helpful information" and "the biggest values." The times are changing, "your Greyhound agent may be a woman travel expert." While a number of themes are part of this advertisement, the main theme of this advertisement is affordability—"the biggest values," and timetables and tariffs "bulging with bargains." *GBM*

Democracy of Goods

"You don't have to be a millionaire to enjoy America's fabulous vacationlands." Playing to the theme of the democracy of goods, this 1950 advertisement suggests that taking an Amazing America Tour is what millionaires do, but thanks to Greyhound, those with a travel budget "no matter how modest" can enjoy equal access to "magnificent National Parks, exciting cities, historic shrines, gay resorts." *GBM*

Starting in the late 1920s, Greyhound advertisements often depicted financially and socially independent women. In this advertisement, addressed "To the Ladies," and most likely in a women's magazine, a group of middle class women of various ages—most likely a family—gaze at a miniature bus symbolizing the real thing and actual travel. *GBM*

This 1947 advertisement offers both the independent young woman enjoying a horseback ride on a Southwestern desert vacation, while a young mother and her daughter pause mid-hill—and mid-thrill—on a toboggan in the snow covered North. *GBM*

Men

Aboard a Greyhound you can relax
Carefree and Comfortable

Step aboard a Greyhound, sink back into one of the deeply cushioned, body-contoured chairs . . . and enjoy the most restful ride you've ever had! It's smoother, more relaxing than even the costliest private limousine—and here's why:

LONG WHEELBASE, PERFECTED SPRINGING, aluminum alloys for strength and lightness . . . these give a steady-level ride impossible in smaller vehicles.

SKILLFULLY DESIGNED SEATS of foam rubber, recline at lever-touch to the most desirable positions for watching the scenery, resting, napping.

ADJUSTABLE FOOTRESTS, with many positions to suit your leg-length or your whim.

CONTROLLED TEMPERATURE, EFFICIENT VENTILATION. Whatever the weather may be *outside* your SuperCoach, it's pleasant *inside*. There's well-regulated

heating when needed . . . continuous circulation of fresh air . . . and, on most coaches, perfected air-conditioning.

SOLEX SAFETY-GLASS WINDOWS, on all the newer buses, allow perfect observation, while filtering out harsh sun rays.

ADJUSTABLE SHADES, FOCUSED LIGHTING. Translucent plastic shades are easily drawn to keep out the sun, while admitting plenty of light. Soft over-all lighting, plus individual reading lamps for each passenger.

INSIDE BAGGAGE RACKS, right above you, for packages, wraps, light luggage. Weather-proof, locked compartments for other baggage.

COURTEOUS, HIGHLY-TRAINED DRIVERS selected for natural ability—schooled and experienced—with unmatched records for safety and dependability!

All these Greyhound features add up to the smoothest, most relaxed ride on American highways.

Congenial, Greyhound passengers relax, nap, enjoy the passing scene.

During the war, Greyhound advertising prominently featured men as members of the military, fighting on the battlefield or working on the home front to bring victory. The soldiers, in particular, paused to dream about the future; with Greyhound making sure those dreams included new buses and terminals. Following the war men are businessmen, salesmen, husbands, and fathers, with all seeming to be part of a family unit. This advertisement features men as part of this post-war focus on domesticity. *HML*

Social Cohesion

"The people you meet aboard a Greyhound somehow seem more neighborly, more relaxed, easier to talk to." In particular, "*Greyhound* has come to mean *Friendly Travel* wherever you may go." This 1951 advertisement uses the same format to promote social cohesion Greyhound used 20 years earlier. A painting has replaced the colorized photograph, but the scene is the same. A bus filled with well-dressed middle class white folks and a small child interacts with an adult across the aisle, an image that reflects the aspirations of the vast majority of Americans. *GBM*

There's something about a GREYHOUND—
that makes it the FRIENDLY way to travel!

GREYHOUND

The Highway Traveler
1946-1952: Postwar

The crisp air of an autumn in New England and the road leads the traveler on, but first a pause in this quaint village. The bus needs gas at the Gulf station while the passengers take a break to relax and perhaps get a snack. All the while the chance to admire the leaves—"the maples are really colorful this year, aren't they." *MBS*

The war, for most, is becoming a distant memory by the autumn of 1949. *The Highway Traveler* offers a view of dude ranch guests around a lunchtime campfire in the Arizona desert—with a stately saguaro cactus as a landmark. This is just the place to visit when the winter wind whips the snow across the plains of the Midwest. Of course, you will go Greyhound to get there. *MBS*

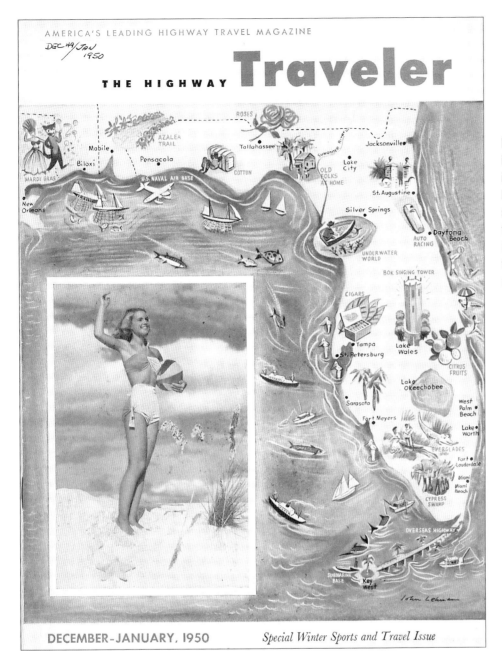

AMERICA'S LEADING HIGHWAY TRAVEL MAGAZINE

DEC 49/JAN 1950

THE HIGHWAY **Traveler**

DECEMBER-JANUARY, 1950   *Special Winter Sports and Travel Issue*

Leaving the Forties behind and starting a new decade, little did most folks imagine that the Korean War would begin in June 1950. A glamorous swim suit-clad young woman offers something we can aspire to be or enjoy seeing when we take the Greyhound and travel to sunny Florida in the winter. *MBS*

Reportage: Tempting the Armchair Traveler

Greyhound benefited from articles in mass circulation magazines written by seasoned professional travel writers. These articles promised objectivity, something that Greyhound's advertisements could not. Potential Greyhound travelers relied on accounts by professionals to validate the claims of the advertisements. "I'm a Vacation Bus Rider," by Don Eddy, appeared in *The American Magazine*, July 1950 issue. Eddy wrote about his 3,000-mile journey by Silversides Super-Coach. Despite Eddy's initial doubts about the trip, he became an ardent enthusiast, indicating it was a "real vacation,

one of the most enjoyable I ever had." He wrote positively about many facets of the trip Greyhound advertising addressed, including the driver, the comfort of the bus, the affordability, the social cohesion among the passengers, and the food. Not everything was wonderful. "Restrooms can stand a lot of improvement," Eddy wrote. "The worst are in small towns." Travel accounts like Eddy's were consistently favorable. What the advertisements promised, Greyhound could for the most part deliver. It was often enough to persuade the armchair traveler to go Greyhound.

TRAVELER TABLEAU: PAUL

Paul is a farmer. In 1950, it is still possible to operate a small farm. A bachelor, he plans to take a much needed vacation from the rigorous demands of dairy farming, with the twice-a-day chores to milk his cows. Thanks to his recent investment in a Surge milking machine, he no longer needs to hand milk his small herd of Guernsey cows. He plans to have his nephew, who can operate the milking machine, take over the chores while he enjoys his vacation. Due to favorable spring weather, Paul has planted his crops. This is his chance for a brief vacation.

An avid reader, Paul enjoyed Don Eddy's article and this assured him that the glossy advertisement in *Life* magazine at right

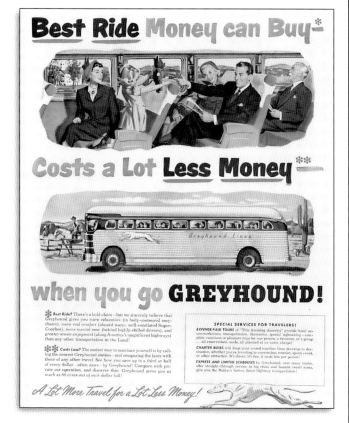

AC

GBM

that caught his eye, was close enough to reality for him to take the Greyhound. He would enjoy the comfortable and safe ride, but he needed to save money and get "A Lot More Travel for a Lot Less Money." Paul sent away for information on the "This Amazing America" expense-paid tours, since he wanted Greyhound to make all of the arrangements once he decided on the four-day tour of Washington, D.C. Paul was excited about the tour since Greyhound noted in its advertising, "The Nation's Capital is center of the 1950 Sesquicentennial Celebration."

Paul also found this advertisement at left helpful since it notes the three nights' hotel in Washington costs only $19.75. He, of course, has already determined the added round-trip fare from his farm home.

AN ANNUAL REPORTS ALBUM 1946-1952

Greyhound's Annual Reports featured covers that management believed best represented the company to its investors, the financial community, suppliers, and those elements of the traveling public. All *MBS*

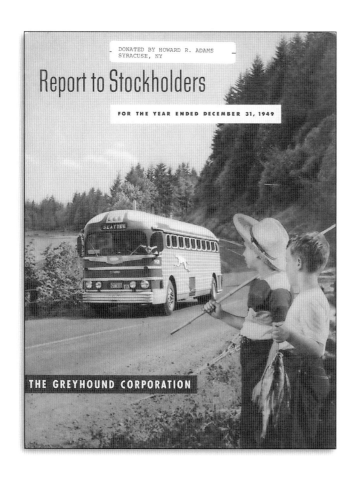

Report to Stockholders

FOR THE YEAR ENDED DECEMBER 31, 1949

THE GREYHOUND CORPORATION

SILVER ANNIVERSARY
1926-1951

THE GREYHOUND CORPORATION
REPORT TO STOCKHOLDERS
FOR THE ANNIVERSARY YEAR ENDED DECEMBER 31, 1951

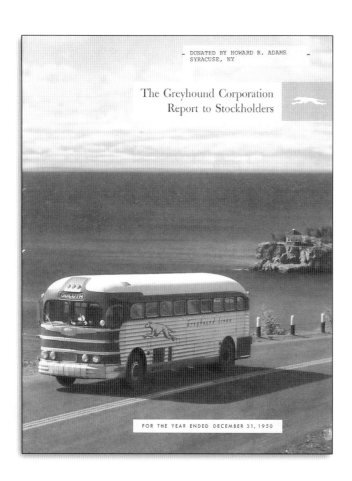

The Greyhound Corporation
Report to Stockholders

FOR THE YEAR ENDED DECEMBER 31, 1950

THE GREYHOUND CORPORATION

Report to Stockholders
for the year ended
December 31 1952

A ROADSIDE ALBUM: 1940-1952

Helenwood, Tennessee. *JD*

Standish, Michigan. *JD*

Tavernier, Florida. *JD*

Glendale, Nevada. *JD*

Angola, Indiana. *JD*

Tofte, Minnesota. *JD*

Arriba, Colorado. *JD*

Big Timber, Montana. *JD*

A Terminal Album: 1940-1952

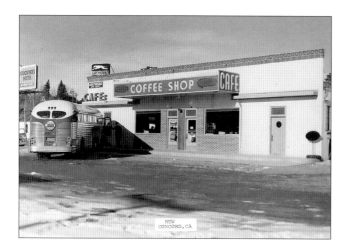

Concord, California. *AACA*

Eau Claire, Wisconsin. *GBM*

Portland, Oregon. *AACA*

Greyhound Key, Florida. *GBM*

Los Angeles, California. *AACA*

Sacramento, California. *AACA*

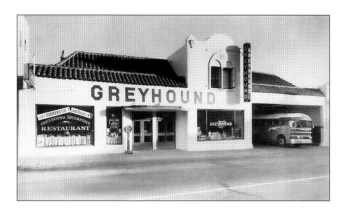

San Luis Obispo, California. *AACA*

La Fayette, Georgia. *JD*

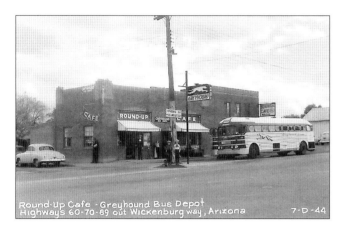

Wickenburg, Arizona. *JD*

Interior of San Luis, Obispo, California. *JD*

Indio, California. *JD*

Modesto, California. *JD*

Chapter Four
1953-1964: Years of Innovation, Growth, and Celebration

The early 1950s began an incredibly creative and innovative phase in Greyhound's history. Greyhound promoted bus travel for the masses. Significantly, it is important to see the company as more than that. The experimental prototype Highway Traveler and Scenicruiser introduced by Greyhound in 1948 and 1949, demonstrated that it was at the forefront of transportation innovation. However, it was not enough to offer attractive images of the future in wartime advertisements and experimental models to entice the traveling public. Greyhound would have to make these dreams come true and offer actual production versions of the experimental models—exactly what Greyhound did.

Greyhound promised a "New Era in Highway Travel," with new buses and terminals, part of a lifestyle open to an ever-expanding number of increasingly prosperous Americans. The public had gotten a taste of the possibilities of this wonderful future at the World's Fair in New York in 1939 and 1940. Three of America's most influential industrial designers contributed to the Fair's focus on the future. Historians credit Walter Dorwin Teague with shifting the focus from a celebration of the 150th anniversary of George Washington's birthday to the Fair's focus on envisioning the future. Henry Dreyfuss developed Democracity, a utopian vision of the future, inside the Fair's Perisphere. Norman Bel Geddes created a 1960 city whose heart relied on arteries in the form of multilane highways—something expected from his client, General Motors, but

AC

a vision well suited to Greyhound's aspirations. In particular, the motto for the inaugural edition of the Fair, "Building the World of Tomorrow," reflected Greyhound's future wartime and postwar efforts.

DREAMS FULFILLED
1953: The Highway Traveler

Greyhound's first installment on fulfilling the promises inherent in its postwar experimental prototypes was the introduction of the innovative production Highway Traveler in 1953. Intended to be the major component in its fleet, the Highway Traveler bore no significant resemblance to the experimental Highway Traveler prototype. Distinctively styled in its own right, featuring a single-level passenger platform, the design of new bus reflected the template established by the experimental X-1, introduced in 1935. The front end foreshadowed the design of the forthcoming Scenicruiser. The body, wrapped in alumilite, featured its most distinctive design feature—four large six-foot long double windows with a tinted glass area more than 50 percent greater than the Silversides Super-Coach.

AACA

Key engineering innovations of the new Highway Traveler included power steering and an air suspension system utilizing eight air bellows—two per each wheel—that eliminated metal leaf springs. Leveling valves kept the vehicle level. Continuing their fruitful collaboration, Raymond Loewy and Associates designed the interior. Pastel tones of tan and brown created just the right ambiance for passengers to enjoy the individually controlled foam rubber reclining seats featuring "dished" backs for greater privacy and less crowding.

Subjectively, the production Highway Traveler did not possess the dramatic departure from existing models that the experimental Highway Traveler embodied. In fairness, the mainstay of the Greyhound fleet would need to be more conservative in its design configuration.

AACA

1954: The Scenicruiser

A large crowd gathered in Pontiac, Michigan, at the General Motors Truck and Coach facilities on July 14, 1954, to witness the 1955 Mrs. America, Wanda Jennings, christen the first production Scenicruiser. According to a Greyhound press release, Greyhound President Orville Caesar presented the bus to Mrs. America, "to symbolize the fact he was presenting the special new bus to American women everywhere." Consider the fact that Mrs. America represented independent, self-reliant American women, a depiction at odds with the usual representation of married women as inseparable from her family. Acknowledging Greyhound's belief in the reality of the future it forecast during World War II, Caesar also declared, "And now finally here is the beautiful new Scenicruiser, which we believe will bring about a new age in highway travel."

Differing somewhat from the experimental prototype, the production alumilite clad Scenicruiser featured the bay window design of the recently introduced production Highway Traveler, single headlights, elimination of the rooftop destination display, different lettering for "Greyhound Lines," and slightly modified bumpers and passenger door windows

AACA

compared to the prototype. The new Scenicruiser utilized power steering and brakes, air conditioning, two diesel engines, and air suspension. Greyhound promoted the Raymond Loewy Associates designed interiors that included a lavatory and accommodated 10 passengers in the lower level and 33 in the upper level.

AACA

AACA

Scenicruiser interior. *AACA*

Scenicruiser driver controls. *AACA*

Traveler Tableau: Evan
Taking the Armchair Traveler for a Ride

Unlike other Traveler Tableaux in this book, this one features an actual traveler—Evan McLeod Wylie who published his account, "I Rode the Super-Bus," in the January 1955 issue of *American Magazine*. Armchair travelers would read about Wylie's 2,000-mile trip from New England to Florida in the new Greyhound Scenicruiser, calling it "the latest thing in luxury on rubber tires." His account gave credence to naming the "fabulous new super-bus" a Scenicruiser. Finding it difficult to contain his enthusiasm about his journey, Wylie declared "Land-

MBS

marks of American history from Washington's Mount Vernon to the old Spain of St. Augustine brought me face to face with stirring chapters in 500 years of New World history. A pageant of America—scenic, historic, romantic America—unfolded before me as we rolled down the highway... ushering a new era in highway transportation."

It is certain Greyhound enjoyed this ecstatic publicity, hoping that Evan Wylie's account would cause folks to get out of their armchairs and take a trip on the new Scenicruiser and enjoy the "New Era" in travel.

1956: New Roads for a "New Era"
The Federal-Aid Highway Act of 1956

In November 1948, *Holiday*, America's most prominent travel magazine, included "Mountain Bus Driver." The account chronicled Don Wharton's Greyhound bus trip across the mountains from Winston Salem, North Carolina, to Charleston, West Virginia, with bus driver Johnnie Jones at the wheel. It was a trip filled with horseshoe curves and one-lane bridges over a winding two-lane road. Wharton

informed readers that a soldier got sick from the ride, and wintertime riders could expect ice and "snowdrifts as high as the bus." Greyhound could take solace in an important message from the article: the trip was without a safety related incident—just one more uneventful trip by the driver now able to add the 267-mile trip to his accident-free 1,093,000 miles with Greyhound.

By the mid-1950s, the two-lane highway was still the rule, not just over the mountains in West Virginia, but across the nation. However, this was about to change. A crucial element for the "New Era" proclaimed by Greyhound was a system of new highways, brought to life by the Federal-Aid Highway Act of 1956. The "New Era" also embodied the significant cultural, economic, and demographic changes affecting the nation following World War II including an expanding population—think baby boom, a higher standard of living, and increased leisure opportunities.

In the 1930s, President Franklin Delano Roosevelt sought to address the problems created by the Great Depression through a variety of programs collectively known as the New Deal. The programs included numerous job-creating public works projects. Interest in the benefits from improving the nation's interstate highway network led to the passage of the Federal-Aid Highway Act of 1938. This law provided funds to study the possibility of a system of national toll roads. The subsequent report concluded intercontinental traffic volume was too low to support toll roads.

Meanwhile, the Pennsylvania Turnpike opened to traffic on October 1, 1940, becoming the model for future interstate highway design. World War II put efforts to establish a nationwide system on hold until 1944, when Congress passed another Federal Aid-Highway Act authorizing construction of a limited 40,000-mile "National System of Interstate Highways" connecting major cities. However, the law did not provide federal funding for construction. In addition, with various states primarily responsible for construction, no uniform design and construction standards existed. With states required to assume major responsibility, construction proceeded at a snail's pace.

War interrupted again; this time it was the Korean War lasting from 1950 to 1953. However, during the war Congress passed the Federal-Aid Highway Act of 1952 authorizing funds for construction—the first such federal allocation—totaling only $25 million,

with disbursement requiring the 50-50 matching of funds by the states. In part, these limited funds accounted for a meager 6,500 miles of improved highways completed by 1953.

Of great significance was the 1952 Presidential election of Dwight Eisenhower, arguably the key catalyst in the establishment of the "National System of Interstate Highways." Historians attribute Eisenhower's strong advocacy for the interstate system to his participation in the 1919 convoy of 81 army vehicles, mostly trucks that traveled from Washington, D.C. to San Francisco, California, a distance of some 3,250 miles, requiring 62 days. The rigors of this cross-country trek heightened Eisenhower's awareness of the military necessity of good roads. World War II gave him first-hand experience utilizing the German Autobahns to move military troops and supplies.

In addition, Eisenhower was among those who saw the civilian economic benefits of an interstate system. In his 1954 State of the Union Address, Eisenhower highlighted his commitment to the interstate system declaring it important to "protect the vital interest of every citizen in a safe and adequate highway system." The establishment of a system floundered as arguments over the allocation of funding between the federal and state governments ensued. In his 1956 State of the Union Address, Eisenhower again urged approval for a "modern, interstate highway system." Finally, later that year, on June 29, 1956, President Eisenhower signed the Federal-Aid Highway Act of 1956 authorizing a 41,000-mile interstate system, allocating $25 billion for construction for the fiscal years 1957 through 1969.

The "New Era" Greyhound proclaimed for its new Highway Traveler and Scenicruiser buses reflected their link to the new interstate highways. In retrospect, we can also see the interstate highways benefited the growing numbers of automobile owners. In the end, the combination of increased automobile ownership and the new interstates would have negative consequences for Greyhound.

1956: A New President

Also in 1956, seizing the mantle of leadership for Greyhound's "New Era," Arthur Genet assumed the presidency replacing Orville Caesar, president since 1946; starting with Greyhound's predecessor, Northland Transportation Company, in 1925. Genet's tumultuous two-year term included the firing of 259 "supervisors below the level of president" and declaring he was making changes that "should have taken place 10 to 15 years ago." Genet's comments suggest the changes he made should have begun as early as 1941, ignoring Greyhound's successful efforts to both cope with wartime conditions and promote the dreams of a bright postwar future that came true in the experimental prototypes and the production Highway Traveler and Scenicruiser.

Genet embraced the "New Era" of travel, seeing the interstate as the road to Greyhound's success. Ignoring both the automobile and the airplane, Genet declared, "The turnpikes are giving Greyhound a new 'super' right of way that permits them to compete with the railroads for long distance passengers." Genet, of course, did not have the benefit of hindsight that now recognizes the affects of the "New Ear" of the interstate: the ever-increasing ownership of automobiles by an expanding and more affluent middle class and the growth of airline travel. Perhaps the Greyhound corporate culture needed to change, but many of the changes Genet made were in large measure based on his questionable analysis of Greyhound's past and the factors that would affect its future. He established Greyhound Rent-A-Car, Inc., quickly seeking to expand service in 122 locations in a year. *Forbes* magazine labeled the overly optimistic effort a "costly flop." The magazine offered additional evidence for his short tenure, noting, "Genet borrowed so freely that by 1958 long-term debt had reached a worrisome 35% of total capital," with losses totaling $6 million. Genet was replaced in 1958.

On a more positive note, Greyhound began a revamping of its food service, modernizing Post House Restaurants and gradually reducing their number, as well as establishing restaurants in Holiday Inns—part of an effort to find new locations based on the new routes on the new interstate highways.

1956 and 1961: The Meaning of Freedom

While not sponsored by Greyhound, a Scenicruiser became the perfect vehicle to tell the larger story of America's history in a Freedom Foundation Special Award winning film, *Freedom Highway*, introduced in 1956. A Greyhound Scenicruiser travels from San Francisco to Washington, D.C. A diverse cast of passengers included an embittered father on his way to Washington, D.C. to accept the Congressional Medal of Honor awarded to his son, killed in action during the Korean War; a teenage Boy Scout; a "mysterious stranger"; and famed country music and movie star Tex Ritter. On the road, each passenger learns valuable lessons about the meaning of freedom in America's past and more importantly in the present. One reviewer declared, "Greyhound Lines and America have never looked so good."

For some Americans, the country did not look "so good." In part, they were Black Americans who were the victims of racial discrimination. Others became part of the Civil Rights movement, an effort to end such discrimination and expand freedoms to Black Americans. The Greyhound bus played a role in one facet of this effort.

Over the years, Greyhound adhered to local laws and customs regarding racial segregation. Throughout the South, Greyhound depots and terminals accommodated separate facilities for whites and "coloreds" known as "Jim Crow". Typical was the Washington D.C. Greyhound Terminal that opened in 1940, featuring "colored" shower rooms, waiting rooms, rest rooms, and restaurant. Greyhound became part of the larger story of the civil rights movement.

On May 4, 1961, civil rights activists began the Freedom Rides, protesting these kinds of segregated facilities. "Freedom Riders" often rode Greyhound buses and at stops attempted to use segregated facilities—blacks to use "whites-only" and whites to use "colored" facilities. They encountered violent responses from white mobs. In Anniston, Alabama, a Greyhound bus caught fire when firebombed. While the Freedom Riders managed to escape from the bus, a mob attacked them. Images of the burning bus and accounts of the beatings filled television news programs and the front pages of newspapers throughout the nation.

Arrived in Washington   *, Leaving for*

OB-H974

GBM

The Freedom Rides did not continue until Greyhound gained the assurance of a police escort for a trip from Birmingham to Montgomery, Alabama, on May 20. However, police abandoned the escort resulting in baseball bat and club attacks on the Freedom Riders. United States Attorney General Robert Kennedy dispatched 600 federal marshals to quell the violence. On May 24, Freedom Riders again rode the bus from Montgomery, Alabama, to Jackson, Mississippi. When blacks tried to use the whites-only facilities, police arrested them, sending them to the penitentiary in Parchman, Mississippi.

Due to the notoriety caused by the violence, later in 1961, the Interstate Commerce Commission ended segregation in all facilities that provided interstate transportation services.

Despite the personnel changes that resulted from controversial management decisions, the "New Era" proclaimed by Greyhound hit a significant peak in 1960. In that year, Greyhound carried an astounding 100,000,000 travelers—something it never attained since. Greyhound offered the finest buses of their day, continuing to take steps to insure this leadership would continue.

Innovation, "The Democracy of Goods," a Real-Live Dog, and an Iconic Slogan.

During Arthur Genet's brief tenure Greyhound reduced its print advertising budget, shifting funds to radio and television advertising. A fondly remembered feature of the new emphasis was the 1956 introduction of Steverino, an actual Greyhound, who would be renamed Lady Greyhound in 1958. The dog most notably appeared on comedian Steve Allen's television show, aired Sunday nights on NBC-TV during the 1957-1958 television season. The dog also made frequent personal appearances, gaining significant positive publicity and goodwill for Greyhound.

Greyhound's commercials on Allen's program also included what is arguably the company's most famous slogan. Introduced in 1956, the slogan offered several variations, retaining its basic message for over ten years. Put to music on Allen's show the slogan became a jingle declaring, "It's a comfort to ride the bus—and leave the driving to us." The double meaning of "comfort" suggested to potential travelers both the quality of the ride in the air suspension equipped buses and the emotional feeling of security with a highly skilled Greyhound driver at the wheel.

Variations of the slogan included: "It's such a comfort to travel by bus—and leave the driving to us" and "It's such a comfort to take the bus …and leave the driving to us." Greyhound applied the popular slogan to its buses as seen in this photograph of the Highway Traveler and the Scenicruiser. A later version replaced "comfort" with "pleasure."

Greyhound's print advertising logically focused on its new Highway Traveler and Scenicruiser intro-

MBS

duced in 1953 and 1954, respectively. Of more than passing interest, and at odds with World War II, an acknowledgement of American participation in the Korean War (1950-1953) is missing from Greyhound advertising.

As noted previously, in *Advertising the American Dream*, Roland Marchand argued the "democracy of goods" refers to the ability of modern mass production and distribution to enable everyone to "enjoy the society's most significant pleasure, convenience, or benefit." Highlighting "low-cost luxury," Greyhound advertising promised the democracy of goods to all.

Marchand also declared that in general: "Advertisements depict and describe the material artifacts available for purchase at a given time. They reveal the state of technology, current styles in clothing, furniture, and other products." Greyhound advertisements combined the "democracy of goods" with depictions of the most modern "current styles." Technological innovation and unmatched comfort and safety became crucial elements in a world of fashionable middle class Caucasians attired in the most stylish clothing and accessories.

Criticism of this focus on the middle class misses the point. Since advertisements are about aspirations, who would aspire to anything less. Greyhound suggested that everyone could at least become a member of the increasingly affluent upwardly mobile middle class. However, the depiction of Caucasians to the exclusion of other racial and ethnic groups, except in supporting or subservient roles, while consistent with advertising in general during this period, needs acknowledgement.

AACA

A vacation by Greyhound

is a vacation from driving...

—with "low-cost luxury" all the way! Now you can take delightfully scenic, wonderfully relaxed highway trips . . . with none of the cares, and only a fraction of the cost of driving! Magic Air Suspension (on the new luxury coaches) actually floats you along in a smooth, vibrationless ride. Sit back in a reclining easychair . . . behind one of the world's best drivers!

Every mile a Magnificent Mile aboard new Air Suspension coaches

Greyhound Scenicruiser®
and Highway Traveler®

Never a dull moment! Huge, softly-tinted picture windows frame dramatic panoramas. Scenicruiser has raised observation level, complete washroom. Both coaches feature perfected air conditioning.

FREE! VACATION PLANNING MAP OF AMERICA

Mail to **Greyhound Tour Dept., 71 W. Lake, Chicago, Illinois.** You can build your own vacation, with this new, full-color map — showing dozens of Tour prices, vacation areas.

Name _____

Address _____

City & State _____

Send me information on an ☐ Individual Tour ☐ Escorted Tour to: _____   HT-6-55

Extra Services, Extra Comforts—all yours by Greyhound

- Free Vacation Planning Service
- Thousands of Air Conditioned Coaches
- Optional Scenic Routes to all 48 States, Canada
- Individual Vacation Tours, Escorted Tours
- Charter Bus Service for Groups
- Package Express Service

An attractive couple took advantage of Greyhound's commitment to "low-cost luxury" to enjoy a glamorous vacation, the democracy of goods come true. Modernism is evident with the innovative "new Air Suspension" equipped Scenicruiser and Highway Traveler that made "every mile a Magnificent Mile." *MBS*

A GREYHOUND ADVERTISING ALBUM
1953-1964

"Five Low-cost Luxury Vacations" reflect Greyhound's promotion of the democracy of goods. The Scenicruiser occupies a prominent spot on a road that improbably runs through the beach. Prominent in the advertisement, one female represents beauty and glamour, while four females represent a variety of roles focusing on the "Living-room Comfort" of the "Complete Washroom" on the "luxurious, dual-level *Scenicruiser*"—the hallmark of Modernism. *MBS*

The increasingly affluent middle class is on display, with a chic well-dressed woman in a bright red dress and hat and black gloves ascending the stairway of the iconic Scenicruiser—literally stepping "up to a bright new look at America" and to a new look through the "new panoramic view" from "high on the Scenicruiser's observation deck." Illustrated tableaux offer a look at the washroom, air-conditioned comfort, and air suspension ride of the "new" innovative Scenicruiser. The democracy of goods presented as "tomorrow's travel luxuries—at yesterday's low prices!" *MBS*

Advertisements often combined a number of small photos and illustrations, creating a variety of tableaux—each providing a vignette or "slice of life" for the potential traveler. A series of tableaux promotes Greyhound's innovative Highway Traveler, illustrating the smoothest ride, air suspension, "Through Service to all America," the "World's Finest Drivers," scenic routes, and "center-of-town terminals"—all of this when you "go Greyhound!" *MBS*

An attractive and fashionable woman relaxes in the new Raymond Loewy Associates designed seat of the Scenicruiser. This advertisement combines the democracy of goods—"low-cost luxury"—and Modernism—air suspension, air conditioning, "reclining easychairs," and the washroom. *AC*

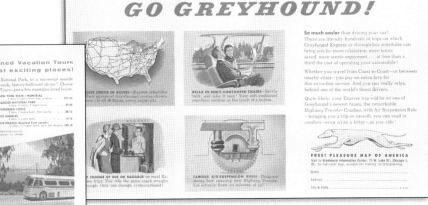

The commitment to improving the nation's highways that would result in the passage of the Federal-Aid Highway Act of 1956, and the new era of highway travel that would result, foreshadowed in this advertisement for "straight through" service with one or no bus and baggage changes across the entire continent. Of course, passengers would enjoy the comfort of air suspension and "body-contoured chairs." *GBM*

This advertisement illustrates Greyhound's use of tableaux based on small photographs and illustrations as well as attractive young women to encourage going Greyhound. *AC*

As shown in these two images, Greyhound used publicity photographs as a basis for advertisements. Men generally appear as bus drivers or part of a couple or family with children in Greyhound's advertisements. *GBS*

Greyhound playing cards. *GBM*

The Highway Traveler 1953-1964

Greyhound's promotional magazine, *The Highway Traveler* continued to feature covers with themes established in earlier issues—attractive scenic vistas and attractive people enjoying dreams come true, thanks to Greyhound.

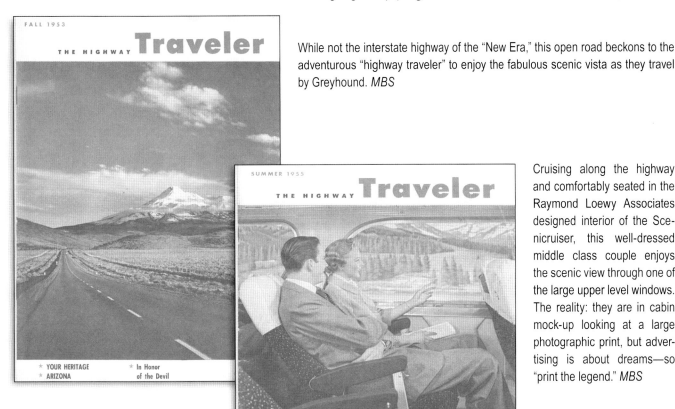

While not the interstate highway of the "New Era," this open road beckons to the adventurous "highway traveler" to enjoy the fabulous scenic vista as they travel by Greyhound. *MBS*

Cruising along the highway and comfortably seated in the Raymond Loewy Associates designed interior of the Scenicruiser, this well-dressed middle class couple enjoys the scenic view through one of the large upper level windows. The reality: they are in cabin mock-up looking at a large photographic print, but advertising is about dreams—so "print the legend." *MBS*

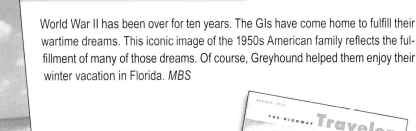

World War II has been over for ten years. The GIs have come home to fulfill their wartime dreams. This iconic image of the 1950s American family reflects the fulfillment of many of those dreams. Of course, Greyhound helped them enjoy their winter vacation in Florida. *MBS*

Spring and "hope springs eternal" for a happily married couple who pause in their gardening to open the mail. Among the seed samples and flower catalog is the "Pleasure Map of America by Greyhound," just the thing to help them plan a vacation going the Greyhound way. *MBS*

A Terminal Album: 1953-1964

By the 1950s, Greyhound adopted the International Style architecture for most of its depots and terminals. Essentially a large box with sharply defined corners, many featured a curtain wall facade of glass and metal spines, while others featured a facade consisting of a series of decorative rectangular boxes and windows. Arguably, all of these depots lacked distinctive design elements that identified them as a Greyhound depot. In fairness, travelers could identify many of these depots because of the large "BUS" sign that included Greyhound's "running dog" sym-

bol. Done in blue and white, the sign's colors were all that remained of Greyhound's 1930s "Blue Period." Atypical is the depot in Pittsburgh, Pennsylvania, featuring a distinctive facade that clearly makes a more assertive architectural statement. The horizontal design elements of the building provide a harmonious contrast to the depot's vertical main entrance section.

Many of the depot buildings housed a Greyhound Post House restaurant and other retailers including other restaurants, cafes, and cocktail lounges.

Fresno, California. *JD*

Tucson, Arizona. *JD*

Las Vegas, Nevada. *JD*

Milwaukee, Wisconsin. *JD*

South Bend, Indiana. *JD*

Chicago, Illinois. *JD*

Pittsburgh, Pennsylvania. *JD*

San Jose, California. *AACA*

Tacoma, Washington. *AACA*

Long Beach, California. *AACA*

Vallejo, California. *AACA*

San Bernardino, California. *AACA*

Bakersfield, California. *AACA*

A ROADSIDE ALBUM: 1953-1964

Greyhound's roadside in the "New Era" was an interesting mix of the old and new. New Highway Travelers and Scenicruisers shared the road with older Silversides. Travelers stopped to eat at establishments that ranged from the latest and most fashionable to nostalgically remembered long-established cafes. Greyhound Post House restaurants often shared space with depots providing greater convenience for travelers. Greyhound still served numerous small towns soon to be bypassed by the growing interstate highway system. Necessary, but not glamorous, were the fuel stops with facilities that often included restaurants or cafes.

Orland, California. *JD*

Gila Bend, Arizona. *JD*

Little Lake, California. *JD*

St. George, Utah. *JD*

Wendover, Nevada. *JD*

Helena, Montana. *JD*

Brule, Wisconsin. *JD*

Gilman, Illinois. *JD*

Niles, Michigan. *JD*

Kentland, Indiana. *JD*

Sierra Blanca, Texas. *JD*

Fannin Springs, Florida. *JD*

Daytona Beach, Florida. *JD*

Hinckley, Minnesota. *GBM*

Mackinaw City, Michigan. *AACA*

AN ANNUAL REPORT ALBUM

Following the introduction of the Highway Traveler and the Scenicruiser, Greyhound featured them on *Annual Report* covers.

All
MBS

1964: Greyhound's Golden Anniversary

Anniversary celebrations afford opportunities to reflect on the past, highlighting the values and beliefs that provided the basis for the actions taken to achieve success. On the eve of Greyhound's Golden Anniversary, *Forbes* magazine addressed what it regarded as the company's greatest "problem"—what to do with the profits "piling up" at a "record-making clip." Things never looked better. It was time to celebrate success.

In 1964, Greyhound published *A Million Miles a Day* to commemorate its Golden Anniversary and offer its own selective version of the company's fifty-year history. The account begins by declaring, "The progress of Greyhound paralleled the progress of our nation because of the fundamental advantages of highway transportation." Hoping to achieve an account of biblical proportions, the brochure proclaims, "In the beginning, Greyhound's pioneers possessed two unique qualities—skill and foresight—which enabled them to mold an auto-livery business into a coast-to-coast network." As result, "Greyhound did not just 'happen' on the American scene. It was created by long and persistent efforts." The brochure's efforts to validate these proud claims began with another assertion: "Greyhound holds the busmanship title of the world." It also offered

a nostalgic look back to 1914, characterizing the time as the "carefree years before and after the First World War" when "Derby hats and stripped jackets were popular attire, and fashionable women wore bird studded hats" and when "housewives were worried about the prediction that skirts would be boosted above the ankle line." While this account contains some truth, it leaves out the hardscrabble world of the Iron Range miner who relied on Greyhound's forerunners.

Greyhound publicists then traced the initial development of the Hibbing to Alice Hupmobile "bus" service created by Carl Wickman and Andrew Anderson that led first to the establishment of the Hibbing Transportation Company, with future expansion that "reached the status of a fever," the "keynote for future operations." The company's expanded service from Hibbing to Duluth provided Greyhound publicists the opportunity to paint a vivid picture of this journey. "In fierce weather the truck-chassis buses bucked and skidded, became mired in mud and snow, and iced by sleet."

In 1916, Hibbing Transportation became the Mesaba Transportation Company. The brochure frames this milestone in terms of the physical effort it took to operate a bus line at the time, claiming that drivers sometimes "had to fight for their fares" or hand crank a cold bus engine. In addition, Greyhound's early founders realized some important facts: "That people wanted and needed bus service; that the bus business was sound; and that more and more people would want to go more and more places."

The brochure framed the meeting of these "wants" in terms of continued expansion and innovation. Orville S. Caesar joined with Wickman to create the Northland Transportation Company and then in 1926, the Motor Transit Management Company. The brochure asserts that the "company's research led to the first major change in bus design—placement of the motor up over the front axle." This is a very questionable claim. It ignores the independent development of the "Safety Coach" by William Fageol, introduced in 1922. It is most unlikely that Wickman or anyone connected with what would become Greyhound would have contributed to the Fageol Safety Coach design prior to 1922.

A Million Miles a Day correctly indicates that in 1930, Motor Transit became The Greyhound Corporation, with the "running dog" its famous trademark. Sticklers might argue that Greyhound's Golden Anniversary should be 1980 with its Centennial celebrated in 2030.

Continuing its narrative, the brochure highlights the role of Chicago's Century of Progress as the catalyst for Greyhound Highway Tours and the establishment of Greyhound travel agencies throughout the United States, Canada, Europe, and South America. Ignoring the experimental X-1, mention is made of the Super-Coach, the "engine in the rear type bus" introduced "in 1934"—actually it was 1935, air conditioning in 1936, and the adoption of the diesel engine as standard starting in 1938. The brochure indicates the first Post House, Greyhound's "chain" of restaurants was established in 1937, accurate to the extent that it was in that year that Greyhound established Greyhound Travel Stations, Inc., but Greyhound publicity first used the term Post House in 1939.

The anniversary brochure also indicated that Greyhound began development of a "dual compartment bus" that would become the Scenicruiser in 1940, with its introduction delayed by World War II. This unfortunately misrepresents the development of both pre-war and postwar Greyhound buses. In 1940, Greyhound introduced the iconic Silversides. Artist's renderings of the Raymond Loewy designed Highway Traveler began appearing in advertisements during World War II, starting in 1944, mentioning scale models soon to become actual buses. This design became the basis for the Highway Traveler experimental model introduced in 1948, with the production version unveiled in 1953. In 1949, Greyhound revealed the experimental Scenicruiser, followed by the fleet version in 1954. While it is likely the war did alter the timeline for these buses, the brochure oversimplifies this important chapter in Greyhound's history.

Postwar highlights leading up to Greyhound's golden anniversary in *A Million Miles a Day* included the "New Era" of highway travel with Lady Greyhound, the famous "Go Greyhound …and leave the driving to us" slogan, and the anticipated 1964-5 World's Fair in New York. Greyhound planned "special tours to the fair site and all internal transportation for 80 million visitors." In addition, the company would have its own "special Greyhound building housing special exhibits, a dramatic turntable theater, and a fully automatic vending restaurant which can serve 20 meals a minute."

Ultimately, the anniversary brochure offered a view linking the past, present, and the future. Greyhound hoped the "simple philosophy of its founders" would characterize its next fifty years: "Faith in the future of highway travel in America." However, beginning in 1961, Greyhound had begun to take steps that would shape its future in ways unrecognizable to its founders, establishing food, finance, and service subsidiaries. These actions foreshadowed the extensive diversification program Greyhound would undertake throughout the latter 1960s and 1970s.

1964: World's Fair

In 1964 and 1965, New York City hosted its second major World's Fair of the twentieth century, held on the same site as the 1939-1940 World's Fair. Following its experiences in past fairs and expositions in Chicago, Cleveland, San Francisco, as well as New York, Greyhound began preparations in 1961, establishing Greyhound at the World's Fair, Inc. This was essential given the significant role Greyhound played providing transportation, food services, and information for Fair attendees.

While providing transportation services to and from the Fair, Greyhound would also provide all internal transportation. The unique Greyhound Escorter provided transportation for up to four passengers on the front bench seat. The operator sat in a separate elevated seat behind the passengers. The cover Greyhound's 1963 *Annual Report* features a glamorous couple dressed for an evening out at the Fair riding in an Escorter. In the background, a Greyhound Glide-a-Ride offered transportation for up to sixty passengers. Both the Escorter and the Glide-A-Ride reflect the modernistic style so popular in the early 1960s. These vehicles served Fair-goers throughout the grounds and to and from parking areas. Greyhound also provided pre-planned and individualized tours of the Fair, as well as providing booths for transportation and sightseeing information.

Greyhound publicity noted "Greyhound will have its own building at the Fair," housing ticket counters, travel and tour information booths, package express facilities, and exhibits about buses and scenic attractions in the United States. In addition, Greyhound planned a 1,500-seat theater and a Post House vending machine restaurant capable of serving 20 meals per minute. Greyhound also provided food services for the Rheingold Beer Restaurant for those seeking an "adult beverage." Overall, Greyhound Fair personnel numbered nearly 1,500.

World's Fair publicity hailed it as the "greatest attraction of the century"—a heady claim given the stature of the earlier 1939-1940 World's Fair. The Fair featured more than 140 exhibit pavilions with exhibitors from all over the world as well as the United States. Religious and service organizations as well as businesses sponsored exhibits. Just as the Trylon and Perisphere became the recognizable symbol of the 1939-1940 World's Fair, the Unisphere, a large unique skeletal globe of the world, became the symbol of the 1964-1965 World's Fair. Unlike the Trylon and Perisphere, this still exists in New York City.

MBS

AACA

AACA

TRAVELER TABLEAU: ANN AND JACK
A TRIP TO THE 1964 NEW YORK WORLD'S FAIR

In 1940, recent newlyweds, Ann and Jack, visited New York to take in the World's Fair. Of course, they enjoyed the marvels of the future on display, talking about the trip for years. While not something they got at the Fair, one of their most treasured mementoes is a set of metal Trylon and Perisphere bookends made by Ann's brother, who worked in a foundry.

Ann and Jack have fond memories of their trip by Greyhound and all the planning and saving they did to make their dream come true. They owned a well-used 1936 Pontiac that, while perfectly suitable for their needs around home, did not seem the best choice for a trip from Colorado Springs, Colorado, to New York and back. For them, going Greyhound made the most sense. They looked over the numerous Greyhound advertisements for the Fair, sending away for information. While it would be just the two of them, they found the brochure that prominently featured the Trylon and Perisphere and a family poised to enjoy the sights of the Fair most helpful.

The trip was especially memorable, since it would be their last big vacation trip until after the war. After returning to their home in Colorado, the necessity of American entry into the war seemed ever more likely. Following the Japanese attack at Pearl Harbor, and despite his claim that he was a committed "land lubber," Jack enlisted in the Navy. Like millions of Americans, Ann and Jack endured years of separation, frequent V-Mail letters their vital link with each other. After the war, Jack came home to "settle down" and raise a family.

Twenty-four years after their 1940 World's Fair visit, Ann and Jack decided to visit the 1964 edition of the World's Fair. While they have a new car—a 1964 Buick Skylark—and the interstate freeway system continues to expand, they heed the advice

World's Fair Bound. *AACA*

MBS

of the famous Greyhound slogan: "For pleasure...go Greyhound...and leave the driving to us." They were surprised, but pleased, that the Scenicruiser they rode featured the slogan on its side.

On a bright and sunny day in May, Ann and Jack arrive at the Colorado Springs, Colorado, Greyhound Depot. There is nothing of the International Style Modernism to entice the mid-1960s traveler. In fact, despite the current magazines and 1964 calendar, the depot has a 1940-like ambiance. Among the magazines for sale, Jack grabbed a copy of the latest *Road & Track* with the new Mustang on the cover, while *Movie TV Secrets* with the Beatles on the cover caught Ann's eye.

Once again, Ann and Jack have a marvelous vacation visit to the World's Fair. The air conditioned, air suspension Scenicruiser does prove pleasurable. At the Fair, they visit pavilions including those hosted by Greece, Argentina, and Sierra Leone. Leading American businesses such as Ford, General Motors, Chrysler, IBM, and American Express offered their version of the "fascinating World of

The Colorado Springs, Colorado, depot in May 1964. *AACA*

the Future." Of course, they rode in Greyhound's Escorter and the Glide-a-Ride—sensible choices given the nearly forty miles of promenades and roadways in the 646-acre Fair site.

Very happy, but also very tired, Ann and Jack were especially grateful to have chosen to leave the driving to Greyhound for the return home. Two special World's Fair visits, both made more enjoyable, thanks to Greyhound.

AACA

Chapter Five
1965-2014: Meeting the Challenges of a New Era in Highway Travel

In its first fifty years, Greyhound became an American icon, successfully persuading travelers to "Go the Greyhound Way." In part, this reflected the more limited options available to travelers. Initially seen as a competitor, studies dating to 1925, conducted by the Great Northern Railroad, demonstrated that the bus and the railroad were in fact complementary modes of transportation, with the automobile the chief competition. Preferring to haul freight, America's railroads abandoned passenger service culminating in the establishment of Amtrak in 1971. While automobile ownership steadily increased, significant numbers of travelers chose the bus and Greyhound, in particular. However, during Greyhound's second fifty years, this scenario changed significantly. While still an American icon, Greyhound sought to cope with traveler's decisions to choose alternative modes of transportation: to own and use automobiles and to fly.

Perhaps symbolized by the sterile nature of the new interstate highway system, a once evocatively romantic landscape, now conquered by technology, became less exciting and adventurous. The "New Era" of new buses and marvelous new highways Greyhound promoted promised an ease of travel; but measured in elapsed time, it offered as author Michael S. Sweeney has observed, "little romance." The expanding more affluent middle class that Greyhound had historically sought to entice increasingly found the automobile the best expression of middle class affluence, individualism, and autonomy. The "New Era of highway travel" that Greyhound hoped would include extensive bus travel became a new era for travel based on the private ownership of automobiles.

The infrastructure increasingly developed to serve the interstate traveler was best suited for the automobile. Bypassing small towns, travelers exit an off-ramp for fast fuel, fast food, and a restroom break. The once unique and picturesque roadside now became a stan-

THE GREYHOUND CORPORATION 1981 ANNUAL REPORT

MBS

dardized collection of nationally known franchises. Part of this evolution resulted from customer demand. McDonald's indicates a significant factor in its "billions served" is the customer's expectation of standardization. "A Big Mac is a Big Mac is a Big Mac" anywhere you stop at the "Golden Arches." The advent of drive-through service caters even further to the "keep moving" mentality the interstate highway promotes.

The postwar move to the suburbs necessitated more automobile ownership. The automobile became a necessity for the commute to and from work in what has ironically become the "rush hour." The car payment, while it could be significant, became an expense required of the new era's lifestyle. A family vacation would include lodging, meals, and payments for attractions; taking the bus could require a significant portion of the family budget. Increasingly, families chose to take their car and save the cost of the bus fares for each family member.

The interstate system's emphasis on saving time also led to an increase in airline travel. If the destination was all that mattered, it was the best travel option. Saving the time for more at Disneyland, for example, became the preferred option. Why spend time on the sterile drive on the interstate highway, when it could be spent enjoying the pleasures of the destination. Travelers in-

creasingly paid more for such benefits. Whatever the cost, the bus could not give the traveler the time lost in transit. The automobile, while it did not give the greater time at the destination, allowed the family to be together. Historian Susan Sessions Rugh addressed this point in *Are We There Yet? The Golden Age of American Family Vacations,* arguing that the automobile became a "home on wheels, an extension of domestic space…a sense of security for the traveling family on the road." Over the years, Greyhound advertising offered social cohesion as a reason to travel by bus. Rugh's point is that the automobile replaced the bus as *the* vehicle to promote the social cohesion families came to desire.

Final GMC Bus: 1966-1967

In a marked departure, Greyhound ordered its last General Motors buses for delivery in 1966 and 1967. Greyhound began its association with General Motors during the Great Depression. In a move that meant the survival of both entities, General Motors agreed to take over $1,000,000 in Greyhound bank debt. In addition, General Motors subsidiary, the Yellow Truck and Coach Manufacturing Company, purchased an interest in C.H.Will Motors Company, Greyhound's initial venture in bus manufacturing in 1930, transferring production of all Greyhound buses to its Pontiac, Michigan, facilities. The photographs contrast the final General Motors Greyhound model with a 1930 Yellow Coach Z-250 Model 376.

MBS

AACA

AACA

A Bus Album

The Mack MV620

While never going into actual production, Greyhound considered this distinctively styled prototype, manufactured by Mack in either 1957 or 1958 (accounts vary), identified as the MV620. Factors in the development of this prototype included Greyhound's worries about the performance of the Scenicruiser and the United States government's concerns about the "nearly monopolistic" market share for General Motors.

AACA

AACA

MCI

In the 1960s, Greyhound made decisive moves to manufacture its own buses, severing all ties with long-established manufacturers. Greyhound established Motor Coach Industries, Inc, an American subsidiary of the Greyhound Corporation, located in Pembina, North Dakota in 1962. Greyhound combined these efforts with Motor Coach Industries Limited, Manitoba, Canada, a subsidiary of Greyhound Lines of Canada, manufacturing buses for Greyhound's Canadian operations as well as selling to other bus operators. Limited production of the MC-5 Challenger began by mid-1963 with "bus shells" (complete painted bodies with finished interiors) shipped from Manitoba to Pembina for final assembly.

Greyhound's decision to end its association with General Motors stemmed from the company's plans to manufacturer its own buses and produce additional buses for sale to other businesses through ownership of Motor Coach Industries. In 1933, Harry Zoltok established Motor Coach Industries (MCI) in Manitoba, Canada. Greyhound of Canada acquired 65 percent of the company in 1948. Ten years later, in 1958, Greyhound acquired the entire

company establishing a manufacturing facility in Pembina, North Dakota. Entering the United States market with the MC-5 Challenger in mid-1963, MCI constructed bus shells that included finished interiors in Manitoba, shipping these to Pembina for final full assembly. By 1971, MCI had become North America's largest producer of intercity buses.

The MC-5 Challenger introduced into Greyhound's fleet in 1963. *GBM*

MC-5 Challenger rear. *AACA*

MC-6X. *GBM*

In 1968, Motor Coach Industries introduced the MC-7 Scenicruiser. The 40-foot long 96-inch wide MC-7 followed the introduction of the experimental MC-6X later referred to as the MC-6. Given permission to run the two prototypes as test vehicles, the V-12 diesel-powered MC-6X featured a non-legal 102-inch width. In contrast, fifty legal 96-inch width MC-7s powered by Detroit V-8 diesel engines were in service by 1969. Overall, Greyhound indicated about 1400 MC-7 models became part of the Greyhound fleet from 1968 to 1973.

MC-7. *AACA*

In addition, Motor Coach Industries offered two modified models of the MC-7 Scenicruiser. The first became the Super 7, introduced in 1971, while the second, the limited production Super 7 Turbocruiser, introduced in 1972, featured an experimental turbine-powered engine. MCI and Greyhound would continue extensive gas-turbine engine development culminating in the MC-8 Turbocruiser.

Motor Coach Industries next introduced the MC-8 Americruiser in 1973. By 1979, Greyhound's fleet of over 5,000 buses included more than 2100 MC-8 Americruisers.

Super 7: 1971. *GBM*

MC-7 Super Turbocruiser: 1972. *AACA*

MC-8 Americruiser: 1973. *GBM*

MC-8 Turbocruiser. *MBS*

One of the power plants that captivated automobile, truck, and bus manufacturers was the gas turbine. Sponsored by the U.S. Department of Energy, Greyhound and MCI introduced its gas turbine MC-8 Turbocruiser in 1973. This program, like every other such effort throughout industry, failed to develop a viable gas turbine power plant.

Greyhound began adding the MC-9 Americruiser 2 to its fleet in 1979. By 1985, Greyhound had added 2000 MC-9s to its fleet.

The buses developed by Motor Coach Industries reflected Greyhound's continued efforts to develop innovative designs that began in the 1930s with the stunning X-1. The experiments with reconfigured widths and lengths, gas turbine power plants, attractive and comfortable interior accommodations, and modern exterior styling embodied the spirit of experimentation and optimistic commitment to the future characteristic of Greyhound's first fifty years. The buses also acknowledged the past, continuing to feature alumilite exteriors, first introduced on the iconic Silversides Super-Coach in 1940.

MC-9 1978-9: Americruiser 2, and interior. *AACA*

Diversification: A Strategy for Survival

One strategy Greyhound employed to cope with the changing nature of travel was to establish a diversification program, creating subsidiaries in food, finance, and services beginning in 1961. Initially, this approach produced large amounts of cash that Greyhound used for additional diversification. For example, in 1969, Greyhound acquired Armour and Company, producers of meat products and Dial soap and deodorant, bringing the total to more than 100 subsidiaries. Greyhound gained 38 percent of its profits from these subsidiaries by the start of 1969.

Continuing to diversify, in 1973, Greyhound acquired the Burn Treatment Skin Bank. However, in 1974, the company reported "disappointing losses" in its cattle and poultry operations. The resources used to carry out Greyhound's diversification program prompts questions about resource allocation. To what extent did Greyhound consider upgrading its terminals and roadside facilities and services, a source of significant and ever-present complaints rather than venture into acquiring the Burn Treatment Skin Bank or cattle and poultry operations?

The bottom line was that the goal of diversification was not to make Greyhound a better bus company, but to insulate the parent corporation from the vicissitudes of the changing nature of travel in the vaunted "New Era of Highway Travel" Greyhound promised in 1954.

These *Annual Report* covers reflect the diversification program Greyhound undertook beginning in 1961. *All MBS*

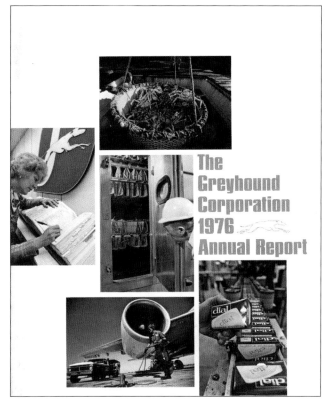

1976

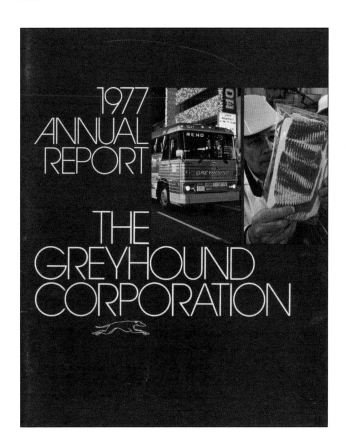

1977

During the 1960s, 1970s and 1980s, Greyhound also sought to link the heritage of the past with its problematic present and increasingly uncertain future. This group of *Annual Report* covers features one of the world's most famous corporate symbols based on the design developed by Raymond Loewy Associates and first used on the Model 719 Super-coach introduced in 1936.

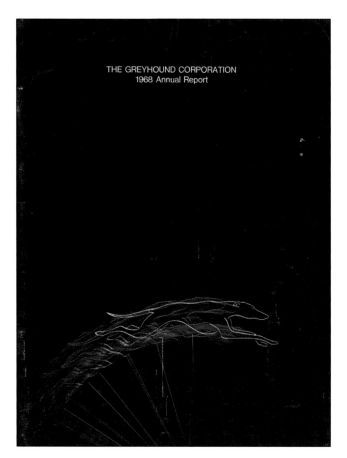

1968

1967

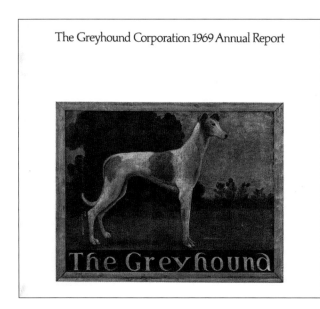

1969

1971

1974

The
Greyhound
Corporation
1980
Annual
Report

1980

1982
Annual Report

The Greyhound
Corporation

1982

Diversification did nothing to alter the steady decline of Greyhound ridership. From the all time high of 100,000,000 riders in 1960, ridership had fallen to 54 million in 1980, reaching an all time low of only 15 million passengers by 1993—15 percent of the 1960 total! A number of significant factors contributed to Greyhound's difficulties. In 1981, the Interstate Commerce Commission deregulated the transportation industry. Greyhound sought such action throughout the 1970s, but in its 1983 *Annual Report* the company attributed its growing difficulties to deregulation declaring, the "new deregulated transportation environment had presented Greyhound Lines with a maze of blind alleys and dead ends." The 1983 *Annual Report* identified Greyhound's matching of reduced fares by "one of our largest competitors" in 1982 that resulted in a $16 million operating loss. The deregulation of the airline industry "spawned dozens of new, feisty airlines…offering fares that were as low as half those of intercity bus lines." Such actions only added to the incentives to travel by air and save money and time—the two crucial considerations in the "New Era." In addition, the same *Annual Report* noted the negative impact of a "47-day strike at Greyhound Lines which effectively wiped out any chance for a profitable year."

Whether mindful of Greyhound's 1954 pronouncement or not, in announcing the sale of Greyhound Lines to a Dallas investor group in late December 1986, John W. Teets, Greyhound Corporation Chairman, declared, "This is the end of an era." The sale acknowledged the fact that Greyhound Lines was just one of many subsidiaries in a highly diversified corporation. Greyhound would continue to operate separately from its long time parent company that would become the Dial Corporation. Diversification did indeed insulate the parent company from a troubled subsidiary.

Within six months, in June 1987, the newly established Greyhound Lines, Inc. purchased rival Trailways Corporation for $80 million. Rationalizing the acquisition, Fred Currey, Greyhound Chairman, spoke about the imminent collapse of Trailways "without intervention." Left unsaid was an explanation of the advantages for Greyhound's decision to spend $80 million on a collapsing rival.

One short-lived asset gained from the acquisition of Trailways was Eagle Manufacturing, Brownsville, Texas, manufacturer of buses for Trailways. By the latter part of 1990, during bankruptcy reorganization, Greyhound sold some assets of Eagle and terminating Eagle production, releasing all production employees. By the end of October 1991, Greyhound retired all Eagle buses from its fleet.

1988 Eagle Model 15.
AACA

Labor difficulties beset Greyhound in March 1990, when all of the drivers, mechanics, and clerical workers represented by the Amalgamated Transit Union went on strike. Greyhound's response was to hire non-union replacement workers. This led to significant violence and property damage. By June 1990, Greyhound had exhausted its cash reserves and filed for voluntary protection under Chapter 11 of the United States Bankruptcy Code, emerging from the process in October 1991.

A review of Greyhound annual reports and public relations statements following bankruptcy reorganization throughout the 1990s reveals a futile search for a meaningful corporate identity and strategy for financial success. A typical comment from the 1996 *Annual Report* declared success "comes from understanding the needs of our customers." Lost on those who sought an effective strategy was the lesson from Greyhound's past when its advertising offered portrayals of what people aspired to be. Essential to such an approach is to substitute wants for needs, persuading potential travelers to want to travel and not just respond to what they need. The cover of the 1997 *Annual Report* declares, "Who Needs Us?" Greyhound ignored aspirations, reminding its customers who they actually were—the less affluent "underserved." Despite news accounts noting the availability of low cost airline fares and the increased role of automobile ownership, Greyhound dismissed these factors: "We know that the biggest competitor for our core customer's travel dollar is not the airlines or even the car, it's the issue of affordability."

In general, Greyhound's concerns in the 1990s focused on survival and the fundamental question: "Who will ride the bus?" These Annual Report covers addressed Greyhound's efforts to find an answer.

1994

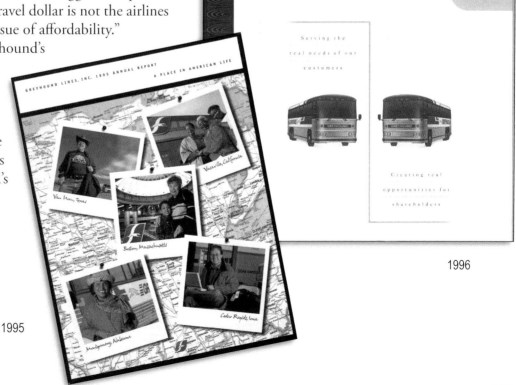

1995

1996

1997

In 1999, Canadian-based Laidlaw Incorporated acquired Greyhound. Laidlaw's 1999 *Annual Report* offered these thoughts about Greyhound, at odds with Greyhound's earlier analysis of its competition: "Greyhound's major competing transportation mode is the family car. Airline discount fare programs can also sporadically affect passenger loads." By 2001, Laidlaw declared bankruptcy, emerging from Chapter 11 proceedings as Laidlaw International in mid-2003. Greyhound continued to operate during this period, but in 2004, in response to its continued financial difficulties, Greyhound made changes that caused significant negative public reaction, announcing measures to downsize and in particular, cut back service in rural areas.

The overall approach of the media was to contrast the current and less than ideal Greyhound with a largely mythical Greyhound, that existed in the imagined past. Responding to the changes Greyhound was making, Jim Pollock, writing in the *Des Moines Business Record* declared he would never ride in a Greyhound, but he fondly remembered the "good old days" with a scene few would consider acceptable today. "In those days you caught the bus at Watson's Grocery Store, a bit of Americana even then. It featured a wonderfully creaky wood floor, beautiful wood cabinets, [and] a spool of string over the counter for wrapping bundles...."

In a sense, Greyhound earned its iconic status because in its first fifty years it offered affordable and accessible travel to millions on innovative buses based on an advertising strategy that created an attractive romanticized reality with word and image portraits offering exciting places to visit and the bus as the means to get there. These were real accomplishments. However, alongside these achievements were the small towns that lacked a depot so you waited in Willard's gas station, roadside stops with restrooms that left much to be desired, and restaurants with forgettable food. Both represented Greyhound, but the best is what we remember, and nostalgia creates a wistfulness about the past, softening the harsh realities until a patina of pleasantness constitutes our memory. It still exists for Greyhound.

Greyhound's ownership as it celebrates its Centennial is the British firm, FirstGroup PLC that acquired Laidlaw International, in 2007. Management quickly began to make substantive changes that reflected a greater understanding of the reasons Greyhound achieved iconic status. It returned to a Greyhound Blue-based exterior color scheme for its buses, offering amenities to attract more than the "underserved." In fact, the addition of amenities and a more elegant exterior paint scheme suggests Greyhound has returned to the formula that helped it achieve success and iconic status. Regardless, Greyhound serves a significantly smaller market from its peak in the 1960s. Greyhound's fleet is currently under 1800—a significant reduction from the peak of over 5000. At present, Greyhound serves more than 3,800 destinations throughout the United States, Mexico, and Canada compared to over 6,000 destinations in the 1960s. Ridership generally is near 20 million per year, with 19 million in 2006, for example.

BL-Photo by Loring M. Lawrence

In response to the increasing popularity of new discount carriers offering curbside service and variable fare offerings, Greyhound introduced BoltBus in 2008 with fares that began with one seat for $1. BoltBus promoted the amenities that included free Wi-Fi, power outlets, and extra legroom on new buses and the safety that a service backed by Greyhound would provide. BoltBus carried 1 million passengers in its first year of operation. BoltBus currently operates a fleet of 103 buses consisting of 71 Prevost X3-45 and 32 MCI D4505 models. Service began in the Northeast expanding to the Pacific Northwest in 2012 and California and Nevada in 2013.

Another service is Greyhound Connect that takes passengers from smaller towns and rural areas connecting them to service in larger urban centers. Greyhound Connect currently operates in Alabama, Arkansas, Colorado, Maryland, Missouri, Montana, North Carolina, and Utah.

BL-Photo by Loring M. Lawrence

The Current Greyhound "Neoclassic Livery" Fleet

BL-Photo by Loring M. Lawrence

Introduced in 2008, these buses all feature what Greyhound identifies as a "neoclassic livery" exterior. The exterior color scheme reflects a contemporary effort to duplicate Greyhound's program to create a harmonious corporate aesthetic in the 1930s utilizing "Greyhound Blue" for buses and terminals. In an effort to attract more up-scale travelers, Greyhound also added amenities to some of its buses including free Wi-Fi, power outlets, extra legroom, leather seating, and three-point seatbelts.

BL-Photo courtesy Motor Coach Industries

Beginning in late 2011, Greyhound contracted with ABC Companies to completely overhaul over 500 of its older MCI 102DL3 coaches. Because the work is undertaken at an ABC facility in Nappanee, Indiana, the reworked work includes a bumper-to-bumper overhaul including new interiors, upholstery, reduced seating that provides greater legroom, WiFi and electrical sockets, wheelchair lifts, LED lighting, overhauled engines and repainting in Greyhound's new blue and grey livery. Coach 6538 shows the result, in Albany, New York in June 2012, alongside a pair of Prevost X3-45 coaches (top image.) Some of Greyhound's G4500 coaches have also emerged from the Nappanee rebuild shop (bottom image.)

In the 1980s, Greyhound offered *Go Greyhound* to the Greyhound passenger. The publication replaced Greyhound's legendary *The Highway Traveler*.

Chapter Six
A Look at America and Greyhound Through the Windows of a Greyhound Bus 1914-2014

GBM

GBM

1914: When the Greyhound story begins, the view of America out the window is from a mostly open-to-the-elements Hupmobile, or later in a home-made body mounted on a truck chassis, bumping along rudimentary roads—perhaps "trails" is a better word—to meet the needs of hardscrabble miners in northern Minnesota. The networks we take for granted today were all in their infancy—the communication network provided the few with telephone service, while the telegraph required trained personnel who knew the Morse code. The railroad network was largely in place; but a national highway system barely existed, even in the minds of a few visionaries, and would take years to create. Bus service is a local business. Greyhound's founders had the vision to see a future network of improved roads out the windshield and the courage to create a company that would grow and help fashion the greatest network of highways in history.

1930s: No one should doubt the devastating impact of the Great Depression, but it is equally important to recognize that the men of vision who operated Greyhound saw opportunities during the Great Depression to innovate, and in the process they fostered

a dynamic corporate culture that developed creative solutions not just survival, but for growth and expansion. They led developments that created revolutionary new buses, creative architecture for terminals and depots, and fostered an overall corporate aesthetic that established Greyhound as an American icon. Greyhound earned its iconic status in the marketplace where the shoals of economic chaos dashed the dreams of thousands of hopefuls.

Greyhound not only survived, but it exuded vitality and optimism about a wonderful future. Greyhound had become, in its own words, a "national

network of lines, cooperating through a mother company which would hold, if not the actual majority, then at least an operating control." Out of the windshield and windows of the bus was an America of limitless possibilities. The marvelous fairs and expositions during the 1930s offered opportunities to dream, but more importantly, they set the stage for many of those dreams to become reality, especially for Greyhound.

World War II: World War II witnessed a tremendous migration within the United States. Millions relocated to new centers for industrial production to meet the demands of war—dislocation and disruption caused by a desire to improve one's standard of living. In addition, millions of service personnel took leaves, came home to visit their families, and returned to military installations. Greyhound "signed up for the duration." Advertisements reflected the wartime priorities—war needs came first.

Whether revamping the system-wide time schedule, seeing over 5,000 of its employees go off to war, or reminding people that wartime needs have prior-

ity over pleasure travel, Greyhound played a key role in helping America win the war. Greyhound transported millions of battle front soldiers and millions of home front soldiers. In addition to this herculean effort, Greyhound continued to dream and to remind Americans of what they were fighting for, in a patriotic advertising program. Naturally, Greyhound promised new buses and terminals, part of the exciting changes to come in an ever more prosperous and peaceful America.

1950s: Greyhound fulfilled the dreams of the war years introducing the iconic Highway Traveler and the Scenicruiser, both fulfillments of the promises made during the war. While just one example of America's unbounded optimism, Mrs. America even christened the amazing new Scenicruiser on behalf of "American women everywhere." The postwar boom was on, the move to the suburbs and with it the promise of ever-greater affluence an attainable dream. Americans were also committed to social change as civil rights issues "rode" the Greyhound bus. The Cold War and a war in Korea did little to break the spell of a belief in the promise of a brighter future. Grey-

hound proclaimed a "New Era in highway travel." Beyond the horizon and not visible through the bus windows, storm clouds were gathering. Greyhound would never be the same.

1960s: Hindsight, always "20-20," tells us it would be a watershed time for Greyhound. While the company envisioned the continuation of the "New Era," with Greyhound the leader, it would not be what Greyhound envisioned. The company would never again attain the 100,000,000 riders carried in 1960. Celebrating its Golden Anniversary in 1964, there was still much optimism. The 1964 New York World's Fair was to be another showcase for Greyhound, a look at a future marked by creative growth and expansion. Instead, these events became evidence of a transformation in America that saw a decline in the role for a nation-wide bus company. The interstate highway system and the roadsides it included were far different from those of the past. Highways were filled with automobiles as Americans increasingly chose to "go by car and leave the driving to me." The destination became the goal, as more and more travelers either drove or flew to spend a week at places like Disneyland. Choosing to manufacture its own buses, Greyhound acquired complete control of Motor Coach Industries, ending its long and successful relationship with General Motors. New MCI buses began to replace the iconic Highway Traveler and Scenicruiser.

1970s: Greyhound's parent company pursued a strategy for survival that made bus operations just one of nearly 100 other subsidiaries. The parent company used diversification to insulate itself from a future that included a significantly smaller market for nation-wide bus service. Despite this strategy, innovation continued to be a Greyhound hallmark. In particular, while ultimately unsuccessful, Greyhound sought to develop innovative bus propulsion systems, working to develop gas turbine engines, introducing the Super 7 Turbocruiser in 1972 and the MC-8 Turbocruiser in 1973.

1980s: Red ink, lengthy strikes, and a devastating fare war hit Greyhound hard. The next move was there, perhaps, to see, if you looked. Greyhound's president established the context: it was "the end of an era." The Greyhound Corporation sold its Greyhound bus line "subsidiary" at the end of 1986. The strategy of diversification allowed the parent company to sell off one of its children…that is, subsidiary. What ended was the connection between a parent company that soon changed its name to the Dial Corporation and Greyhound Lines. In an ever-decreasing market for intercity bus travel, Greyhound Lines, Inc. continued, even purchasing a nearly moribund Trailways in 1987.

1990-2007: In March 1990, a strike by members of the Amalgamated Transit Union began and by June 1990, Greyhound declared bankruptcy. Despite

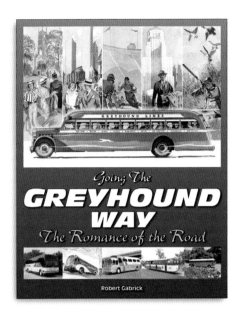
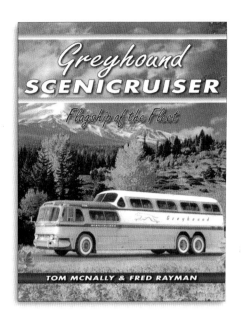

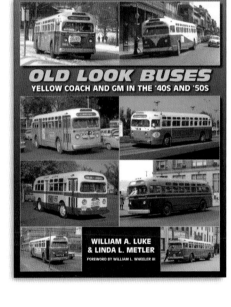
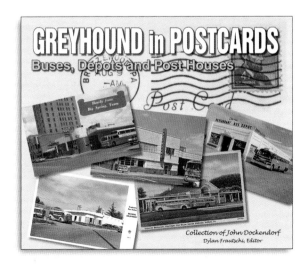
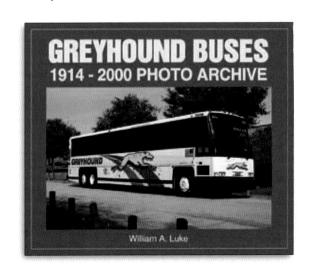

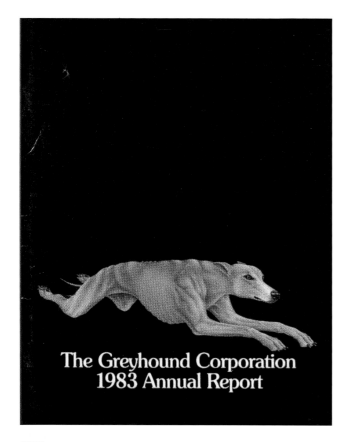

MBS

emerging from bankruptcy proceedings in October 1991, the rough road for Greyhound continued with more losses and a further decline in ridership. It seemed that each year brought a new effort to explain the red ink and to redefine the company. In 1994, "tradition would not be enough, while in 1995, what was needed was a "return to the basics" and going back to Greyhound's "roots." In 1996, the quest was on to "understanding the needs of our customers." In 1997, the big concern was the "issue of affordability." In March 1999, Laidlaw Inc. acquired Greyhound, but by 2001 Laidlaw filed for bankruptcy, reemerging in 2003.

Much to the chagrin of the media, the retrenching continued with reductions in the size of the bus fleet and destinations served. It was as if Greyhound had broken a sacred promise to America—never mind that fewer American's were "Going the Greyhound Way." In 2007, FirstGroup acquired Laidlaw International and took steps to rehabilitate a tarnished icon.

2014: The story of America is in large measure the story of the restlessness of the American people. While the view out the window of today's Greyhound bus offers a very different America from 1914,

GBM

Greyhound survives, continuing to be an American icon. The current ownership, FirstGroup, has sought to return the luster to Greyhound, creating an upscale provider of bus service to passengers who are entitled to enjoy the amenities of such service. While passengers may include the "underserved," no one at Greyhound will tell them that is who they are. They are what Greyhound promoted in the past—people with aspirations to become something better. The one-hundred-year history of Greyhound has witnessed the company's crucial role in the transformation of the nation. While that role has diminished from the peak years, Greyhound still plays a vital role in serving the transportation needs of the nation. Travel on a Greyhound bus will continue to transcend the ordinary, a larger-than-life icon always ready to respond to the never-ending restlessness of the American people.

BL-Photo courtesy Motor Coach Industries